Ordinary Men, *Extraordinary Heroes*

ORDINARY
MEN
EXTRAORDINARY
HEROES

DEXTER YAGER
AND RON BALL

Published by InterNet Services Corporation
USA

Library of Congress Cataloging-in-Publication Data
Yager, Dexter
  Ordinary men, extraordinary heroes / Dexter Yager and Ron Ball.
    p.   cm.
  ISBN 0-8423-4593-0
  1. Men—Religious life.   2. Husbands–Religious life.   3. Fathers—
Religious life.   4. Men—Conduct of life.   5. Husbands—Conduct of
life.   6. Fathers—Conduct of life.   7. Christian life—1960-
I. Ball, Ron.   II. Title.
BV4843.Y34   1992
248.8é42—dc20   92-29994

Printed in the United States of America

99   98   97   96   95   94
9   8   7

To the memory of
Ella Jane Yager Bonvicino:

My dear sister, you were such a loving soul.
You were an example to many through your witness of love
for others and your serving attitude toward us all.
Dexter

You were a model of a strong family life and a good
marital relationship, a Christian wife and mother
whose serving example touched us all.
Ron

THIS BOOK CAN CHANGE YOUR LIFE!

Often when reading a book, we fully decide to apply what we need to our lives. All too often though, weeks later, we have forgotten our good intentions. Here are 5 practical ways to turn good intentions into practical habits.

1. **READ THIS BOOK MORE THAN ONCE.**
    Let me encourage you to personalize and internalize these principals which have generated a turning point in the lives of many people by reading from cover-to-cover, then at least once again.

2. **UNDERLINE AND MAKE NOTES**
    Have a pen and a highlighter in your hand. Underline specific lines and paragraphs – a simple act that will triple your retention rate. Write your own thoughts in the margins and make it your book.

3. **RE-READ YOUR UNDERLINES**
    By underlining and highlighting, you can quickly review key items and portions of this book. Then re-read your key items over and over.

4. **APPLY THE MATERIAL IMMEDIATELY**
    There is an old saying, "Hear something … you forget it. See something … you remember it. Do something … you understand it."
    Apply what you learn as soon as you possibly can … it helps you understand and remember it.

5. **PRIORITIZE WHAT YOU WANT TO LEARN**
    Select 1-3 things from the book, apply them faithfully and make them a habit.

    Remember every person alive struggles with turning their good intentions into habits. Using these 5 points will turn wishing into doing and into habits.

    As I mentioned earlier, many successful people in the past have traced a new, exciting, profitable chapter in their lives to the reading of a specific book. I want that to happen to you!

Write the date you start reading this book: _____

May the date you have just written be the beginning of incredible blessings, rewards and growth!   *— Dexter R. Yager*

CONTENTS

Chapter 1

POSITION AVAILABLE: HERO

One evening not long ago, Ron and I were watching a TV program with his daughter Allison. It was a preview of the summer blockbuster movies soon to be released. One of the films reviewed was *Robin Hood: Prince of Thieves.* This was one movie I wanted to see myself—the legend of Robin Hood has always intrigued and fascinated me.

As we watched this preview, we saw glimpses of the movie's wonderful action scenes. I've always liked that camera shot used in the commercials for *Robin Hood*— where the camera takes an arrow's-eye view as it shoots fifty yards into a tree. Kevin Costner, as Robin Hood, went through his paces and demonstrated his leadership, physical prowess, and courage.

> *The true hero, like Robin Hood, relies on his ingenuity, his natural abilities, and his determination to overcome the odds.*

After the preview scenes, an analysis of the film was narrated by another actor, Pierce Brosnan. Brosnan presented his interpretation of the Robin Hood legend, and he related inside information as to how the movie was made, along with some favorable comments about Kevin Costner.

At the conclusion of the broadcast, Brosnan added something really profound. He said, "We still look for heroes." It was just a passing comment, and most people probably didn't pay any attention, but it stuck in my mind.

We still look for heroes.

Why is it that after eight hundred years the Robin Hood legend is still strong? Why after eight centuries are we still fascinated by this guy?

Ron and I talked about some of the characteristics of Robin Hood. He was courageous. He was decisive. He held strong principles of what was right and good. He exhibited honorable behavior. He was attractive and had great charisma, yet he bonded faithfully with one woman for life.

Why are people still fascinated with Robin Hood today? It's because we are drawn to men who do great things. We're fascinated by the man who rises above the crowd and makes his mark as a hero.

A recent national poll revealed that 60 percent of all Americans believe that there are no longer any heroes. When you think about it, this makes sense: many of the people we used to hold in high esteem in the arenas of public life have fallen. We've seen corruption in government, the failures of our educational system—the list is endless.

> *60 percent of all Americans believe that there are no longer any heroes.*

More than ever, people need heroes.

The Heroism of Individual Men

Ron tells the following story of a real hero:

On March 1, 1815, a small British vessel sailed quietly to dock in a small town on the French Riviera. The dramatic moment had finally arrived. In the early morning hours a solitary figure stepped from that boat onto European soil, and the continent trembled. The word went out, "Napoleon is back."

He had been exiled. He had a disastrous Russian campaign. His grand army had been shattered. He had fled in shame and panic back to his capital in Paris, where great forces had combined to force him into abdication. He had attempted suicide. He carried in a pouch around his neck a concoction of herbs, including the lethal poison belladonna. And he took that poison into his mouth, swallowing it. He had convulsions and stomach spasms, became very ill—and then recovered!

The poison didn't work. Napoleon's physician refused to help him any further. His physician said, "I have sworn the Hippocratic oath to take no man's life. I will not become a murderer. I will not help you."

Soon thereafter Napoleon had recovered his emotional balance but was exiled to the island of Elba in the Mediterranean. He was exiled supposedly for life, but he had eluded his British captors and taken one of their own ships. Now on March 1, 1815, he was returning to Europe to terrorize the whole continent again.

What happened then is one of the great moments of human history. Napoleon made his way through France to Paris. The king on the throne, who had taken his place, fled for his life, abandoning the capital.

Many throughout Europe were terrified of Napoleon's power, and one man emerged as the leader to stop Napoleon. This one man had allies from Prussia, Austria, Russia—other nations lent him their troops and their commanders—but the eyes of the civilized world rested on this one lone figure. That man was the Duke of Wellington.

Wellington was a famous military hero from Britain, a man who had sworn to stop Napoleon. He vowed that no longer would Napoleon terrorize the European continent.

The ensuing battle—the Battle of Waterloo—is one of the most famous battles in all of human history.

But there's an interesting detail that preceded the battle. The Duke of Wellington was in Brussels making preparation. A conference had convened on how to stop Napoleon. The Duke was taking a walk one day through Brussels Park with Thomas Creevey, a member of the British Parliament. They discussed all that would be necessary to bring Napoleon to defeat. While they discussed all these important matters, Wellington saw a statue in the park. Standing before it was a British redcoat, an infantry private. The two men watched in silence as this redcoat, probably from a small town, gazed at this statue. After a few moments Wellington quietly said to Creevey, "There, look at him. It all depends on that article, that man, whether we do business or not. Give me enough of it and I am sure."

Wellington believed in the heroic proportions of the British infantry. He believed they would come through and would stop Napoleon. It depended on the commitment of individual men. "Give me enough men like him," he was saying, "and I am sure of victory."

We feel incapable of fighting not only the big battles in our country, but even the big battles in our lives—controlling our appetites, providing for our families, protecting and educating our children.

On June 18, 1815, at 11:25 A.M., the Battle of Waterloo commenced. It raged until 10:00 that night. Wellington had 67,661 men with 150 artillery pieces. Napoleon faced him with 71,947 troops and 246 guns. Napoleon, maybe out of arrogance and ego—no one is quite sure—decided on a frontal assault, into the teeth of the British forces. The British and Austrians and Prussians fought valiantly, but ultimately all hopes were pinned on the British infantry. The infantry held, made up of men such as that lone private in Brussels Park gazing at a statue in a strange, foreign city.

Napoleon was stopped. The balance of power was saved in Europe. A tyrant fell.

Becoming a Hero in Your World

How can you be a Wellington and stop the Napoleons in your world?

The first step is to overcome your thoughts and feelings of despair. When people say there are no heroes today, it's said out of despair and helplessness. As men especially, we feel incapable of fighting not only the big battles in our country, but even the big battles in our lives—controlling our appetites, providing for our families, protecting and educating our children.

Yes, it's hard to see how anyone can be a hero in today's world. But was Robin Hood's plight any more encouraging? Was Wellington's task any less hopeless?

A true hero is not a superman figure, one who has extraordinary powers to overcome any conceivable problem. A true hero is the ordinary man who has ordinary powers to overcome big obstacles. The true hero, like Robin Hood, relies on his ingenuity, his natural abilities, and his determination to overcome the odds.

As we have pulled together our thoughts for this book, one idea has stood front and center. It's really very simple. In our world today there are many positions open for the job of hero. The requirements for this job involve ordinary skills but lots of determination. It's a job that very much needs men to apply. And it is a job that starts at home.

> *Realize that your most important battle is to be fought over the preservation of your family.*

That's the second step to becoming a hero in your world: realize that your most important battle is to be fought over the preservation of your family. Your home is your battleground. It's a field that many Napoleons march across—Napoleons of immorality, of despair, of unethical behavior, and the twisted values of TV, movies, and today's self-centered culture. Your family needs a Wellington to lead it and to be an example.

You can be a hero to your family. It may be the most important thing you'll ever do.

How to Be a Hero to Your Family

I have, with Ron's help, put together in this book many ideas and suggestions, some that come out of my seminars, some that come from Ron's talks, and many that come from our discussions together. Out of all of this emerge key concepts that we think are vitally important to you.

As you read this book, remember one thing: *Being a hero to your family doesn't always mean that you'll feel like a hero.* Radio personality and commentator Paul Harvey once said:

> *A father never feels worthy of the worship in a child's eyes. He's never quite the hero his daughter thinks, the man his son believes him to be, and this worries him, sometimes. So he works . . . to smooth the rough places in the road for those of his own who will follow him.*

Continue to lead even when it's tough. Your leadership will pay off in the lives of your children.

We believe there is a hero in you, just waiting to be released. Your heroism does not depend on you solving national problems or becoming a famous person in the world. It depends on you becoming the man you want to be, on being present in body and spirit with your wife and children, and on your conducting your life in a way that can be a model for those around you.

> To exist is to change; to change is to mature; to mature is to create oneself endlessly.
>
> **Henri Bergson**

Chapter 2

EIGHT PRINCIPLES OF MALE MATURITY

A hero must first overcome his own immaturity.

Ron recently came across a training manual that explained how to conduct a job interview. In that manual the author said, "The greatest obstacle to executive success is personal, emotional immaturity."

I believe that is also the greatest obstacle to your becoming a hero to your family. You must overcome your own personal immaturity in order to become the man—husband, father, and leader—that your wife and children need.

Marks of Immaturity

In that same manual, compiled and organized by John Wareham, a business consultant, he says that there are four basic signs of immaturity in a job applicant:

1. A pattern of unwise ventures. The immature executive gets involved in situations that frequently don't work out—simply because he didn't plan, was impulsive and undisciplined, and plunged in without thinking. While everyone fails from time to time, the immature executive shows a pattern of failure. His immaturity carries him into situations he can't control.

> *The immature executive is someone who is out of control in his business dealings.*

In the NBA basketball playoffs, a few years back, a guard for the Boston Celtics brought the ball from the backcourt into the frontcourt against the Cleveland Cavaliers. The Celtics hadn't scored in a while, and the guard was anxious to move the ball into a scoring opportunity. He pushed the play a bit too quickly, driving into the lane a bit faster than he could dribble the ball. As he sailed into the air toward the basket, he lost control of the basketball, which, embarrassingly, wound up behind him. The commentator said, "He was out of control. He should have slowed it down and set up for a play."

The immature executive is someone who is out of control in his business dealings. His pattern is one of unwise ventures—like attempting a shot without having the basketball.

2. Living in fantasy worlds. "In your thirties, if you abuse your body, ignoring the warning signs of poor health, in your forties you will pay." Many men live in a fantasy world regarding their health.

Many men live also in a financial fantasy world. You may abuse your finances, and your debt may be out of sight, and you may still convince yourself that everything is going to be just fine. But you're living in a fantasy world unless you seize the situation and take financial control.

3. Failing to deal with pressure rationally. Responding with an explosion of violent temper is clearly an immature pattern. Some men respond to pressure by withdrawing emotionally. We know that at times the pressure is terrific and the intensity great, but you need to learn how to handle this in an adult manner.

By the way, we can testify to the fact that in our life what has made the difference is our faith in Jesus Christ. This spiritual dimension is like a great pressure valve. The Bible talks about the gift of self-control. You can draw on the power of Jesus Christ. He will help you overcome the pressures in your life.

4. Blaming other people for what goes wrong. Finally,

Wareham says not to hire the man who diverts responsibility and blame to others. The immature man fails to take responsibility personally. Roy Smith has said, "The ability to accept responsibility is the measure of a man." When you see someone who makes excuses and diverts blame to others, you are looking at an immature pattern.

> *The immature man fails to take responsibility personally.*

Wareham's warning signs are a good start, but Ron and I would like to expand his list, accentuate the positive, and apply these concepts to home and family life. In order for you to become a hero to your family, you need to discover the essential marks of maturity.

Marks of Maturity

1. The principle of managing the volcano. Picture a volcano—a mountain of fire and lava, steam and hot rock—erupting suddenly and violently, endangering the population surrounding the base of the mountain.

That's exactly what you do when you don't find appropriate ways to let off steam. You erupt, endangering the people around you emotionally and spiritually.

Ron tells the story when he was counseling a young couple some time ago. They were typical of many couples he's counseled. They each wanted to tell him their side of every argument they'd had with each other. They began to have a full-scale argument in front of Ron, and for a few minutes they seemed to forget he was in the room.

He looked at them, and he says it was as if suddenly he no longer saw a man and woman standing there. He saw two volcanoes erupting. All they were doing was spewing hot, fiery complaints on each other.

Gary Smalley is a well-known marriage and family counselor. Ron has read and enjoyed a number of his books and considers his material to be excellent. Smalley says that most conflicts between a man and his wife can be classified as either *offenses* or *misunderstandings*. Offenses occur when one person intends to hurt the other person. Misunderstandings occur when there's miscommunication—but there's no intention to hurt. Smalley says you don't handle an offense and a misunderstanding in the same way. You handle an offense with an apology: "I'm sorry. Forgive me. I wish I had never said that to you." A misunderstanding needs an explanation: "I didn't know you took it that way. Here's what I really meant."

An offense needs an apology. A misunderstanding needs an explanation.

In his book *If Only He Knew* (BK350), Smalley writes about the "complaint box." A couple had come for counseling, and they were having a furious struggle. They fought constantly and were like volcanoes spewing complaints on one another. The counselor instructed them to make a box and put on the box the word *complaints*. He wanted them to take a couple of days and write down on cards each complaint they had about each other. And then they took all of these complaints and put them in the complaint box. So the husband and wife scribbled and wrote furiously and put all of the complaints into the box. And finally the day arrived when the counselor told them to open the box. The wife and husband went into a room—just the two of them—and took off the lid of the box. The wife said she wanted the husband to look in first. There was a divider in the box, so his complaints were on one side and hers on another.

He took out one of her complaints against him: "You don't take the garbage out unless I nag you." Then another: "You leave underwear hanging in the bathroom."

Then it was her turn. She reached into the box, pulled out a handful of cards her husband had written, and read the first complaint: "I love you."

She was startled, but put it aside, pulling out the second card. "I love you." She pulled out another. Again: "I love you." Overcome with emotion, she finally looked at her husband and said, "I love you too. I'm sorry for all that I wrote, all that I said. Some things do bother me, but we'll try to work them out. And yes, I love you too."

Here's the point. That man could have been a volcano of complaints, but he made an intelligent decision. He decided to use that counselor's program as a way to demonstrate to his wife his true heart feelings for her. No wonder she responded to him. Do you wonder why your wife responds to you so happily at times? It's because you have encouraged her, supported her, and loved her. You've been a man who wins with your wife. You've learned to depressurize in appropriate ways, and you have avoided erupting as a volcano of complaints.

> *Don't let yourself become a volcano of complaints. Managing the volcano is a sign of male maturity.*

Ron read a humorous story recently of a woman and her husband who had been complaining. They had bitterness and conflict in their relationship. The man went to church and heard a great sermon about committing one's life to Jesus Christ and applying that spiritual relationship to one's marital relationship. Overcome with emotion, this man made a commitment. He sent his wife red roses, came home early, and brought her a box of delicious gourmet chocolates. When he walked in, beaming and smiling, he said, "Sweetheart, I love you. I'm so happy to be home. I have a surprise. I want to take you out to dinner. I want this to be your night." His wife burst into tears and said, "I can't believe this! You wouldn't believe the kind of day I've had. John fractured his toe. Marilyn failed her algebra test. The washing machine broke twice. And now you come home drunk!"

Make sure your loving behaviors aren't so rare that when they happen, they take your wife by surprise! Don't let yourself become a volcano of complaints. Managing the volcano is a sign of male maturity.

> *Make sure your loving behaviors aren't so rare that when they happen, they take your wife by surprise!*

2. *The light-up principle.* You come home, you've had a stressful day, and you're tight with tension. You walk through the door, and the first thing you do is pour your tension onto your wife and children. That's the dynamic of tension transference. They become tense and follow your lead, transferring the tension they experienced that day back onto you. Suddenly there is a cycle proceeding through every member of the family. Tension transference begins to fill your family with frustration and dread. And *you* have fueled it.

This is a common sign of male immaturity. But you can turn it around.

The flip side to this is something that Gary Smalley calls the "light-up principle." He tells the story of a psychology professor, an elderly gentleman who had been teaching for a number of years. His class decided to play a trick on him. The professor was a man of habit. When he walked into the class, he always went to the same spot, the lectern, and he always gave his lecture in the same way, always concluding at the same time and leaving at the same moment.

So the class came up with a plan. The next time the professor walked in, everyone intentionally looked bored. They didn't even look at him. When he walked behind the lectern, he tried to give his presentation, but they looked even more bored. It was worse than when he walked in. Looking very puzzled, the professor stepped in front of the lectern. Suddenly, about a third of the students began looking at him, the rest still ignoring him. He moved closer to the side and a few more students turned. The professor became more animated, his excitement level rising. He walked over and sat down on a radiator. At this point the whole class riveted their eyes on the professor. They acted absorbed in every word that the professor uttered. He gave one of the best lectures of his career.

The next day the same pattern was repeated. The prof entered the class, walked up to the lectern, and saw a sea of bored faces. He edged to the side, and a few students raised their eyes to his. He edged closer to the side, and a few more noticed. He went to the radiator and sat down, and again the whole class became attentive.

After several days of this, the professor, when he walked into the room, didn't even go near the lectern. He immediately walked to the radiator, giving his whole lecture from there.

Through this technique, the class illustrated the "light-up principle." When he did what they wanted him to do, they would light up. And like a magnet, he was drawn to them, their attention, and their energy.

> **Light up when you see your children, and they will be drawn to you.**

That's the way you should be with your wife and children. When you see her, light up. She will want to be with you. Light up when you see your children, and they will be drawn to you. They will want to be with you and will enjoy your company. You will convey to them that they are so special to you, you light up when they enter the room. Light up your home. Light up your family.

I have also worked to show my wife, Birdie, and kids that they are special to me. They motivate me to succeed. They light my fire to win. I want to light their lives in return with my achievements.

Tension transference is an immature pattern many men act out at home. You can turn it around through the light-up principle. Don't dump your tension on your family, but rather give them your attention and interest.

3. The tuning-in principle. A counselor was talking with a woman client about problems in her marriage. The counselor asked, "What do you want most in your marriage?"

She replied, "I want my husband to talk to me."

After several sessions she returned to the counselor and said, "I have a brilliant idea. I know now how to get my husband to talk to me. But I don't know if my idea will work."

The counselor encouraged her. "Of course it will work," he said.

The woman finally revealed her plan. "My idea," she said, "is to turn me into a television. Then he'd pay attention to me."

But many men focus on TV instead of their family.

Of course, the counselor looked at her, startled and baffled.

The woman went on to say, "You see, that's the only thing he pays attention to. If I could be a television, I'd at least have a chance."

Now I'm not saying all men are addicted to television. In fact, if you're building any kind of life at all, you've broken that bad habit and you're using your life productively. But many men focus on TV instead of their family. Or maybe it's something else, such as sports: "If only I could turn into a football team or a baseball team, then my husband would pay attention to me again."

This is a common sign of male immaturity. It's the tuning-in principle. A man deliberately tunes in certain things, deciding what he will give his full attention to. Of course, that means he also is tuning *out* other things—or people, such as his wife and children.

> **We give our attention to what we want and like and withhold our attention from the people we love but whom we take for granted, even though they depend on us and want a relationship with us.**

Recently, Ron was in the northeast speaking at a business convention. His daughter, Allison, was in rehearsal for a play. He was gone for most of her early rehearsals, and arrived home from his trip late on a Sunday night. He was tired. He had some final business to take care of, some paperwork to do, and so he spread his work out on a table. Allison was so excited about her part in the play, and she came to him, saying, "Oh, Dad, let me tell you about my part. Let me show you what I learned." He told her he was still busy, still working, and didn't have time. But Allison kept asking him to watch her. And finally, impatient, he said sternly, "No, Allison. Stop that. I don't have time right now." He says he even remembers feeling proud of himself, thinking, *I'm really getting to be better at business. I'm not letting this interfere with these important things I have to do.*

But then he tells how he happened to look up and saw his rejected Allison out of the corner of his eye, and he realized he'd done something very wrong. He had tuned her out. Sure, he was tired. But he knew very well if someone else—a business associate—had walked through the door that night, his exhaustion would have vanished. He would have given to that person his complete attention. He says about that incident, "I had failed to give my attention to my own daughter, my flesh and blood, who needed just a few minutes from her dad. It was wrong and unfair."

The next day Ron went out of his way to make it up to her. He went to her rehearsals even though he had a pile of work to do. He decided to tune into his daughter's needs and to tune out his work pressures. He was then so energized that he finished twice as much work as he had previously done.

Now, as the Bible says, there's a time for everything under heaven. There is an appropriate time for work and for play and for family. But too often men do what Ron did that night. We give our attention to what we want and like and withhold our attention from the people we love but whom we take for granted, even though they depend on us and want a relationship with us.

Early in our family life, I began to take all my children on trips with me. I wanted them to learn business from real life.

We started with a Cadillac. Birdie and I would cram all seven kids with us into the car and travel from meeting to meeting. We had great closeness! Everyone was relieved when a motor home replaced the car.

Sometimes I couldn't drive any further, so we would stop for a day in a rest area. Birdie and I would sleep while the kids played. They admit today that they often fought boredom, but we were together.

Harsh words produce hard hearts.

4. The principle of verbal respect. Ron has noticed something over the years in counseling that has made him really concerned. As he listens to couples in counseling situations, he hears them speak to one another with verbal savagery. They wound and cut and slash with their words. Ron knows of one situation where a wife and husband were struggling to communicate. The man was stubborn and unresponsive, and the woman poured her heart out to this man. She had married and trusted him and had borne his children. And finally, she looked at this man who had attacked her so savagely, shrugged her shoulders, and said, "Don't you see? I need your help, not your mouth." The man was startled and for the first time in the situation had nothing to say.

The Bible says that slander, insults, violent language, and verbal attacks must be put away from you. The Bible says to take those things and get rid of them. We believe God will help you with that if you will let God help you. Verbal savagery must stop.

There are two reasons why you need to treat your family with verbal respect. First, because harsh words produce hard hearts. You wonder why your wife is not responsive to you. Could it be that you have wounded her and hardened her heart with your harsh words? Ron sometimes says that he would not talk to a dog the way he's witnessed some men talking to their wives. Harsh words

Verbal stabbing produces bleeding children.

produce hard hearts. When a man learns the art of negotiation in business, he learns not to use harsh language, or be deliberately provocative, or to provoke the other by unnecessary harshness in his language. If that's true in confirming a business deal, it is vastly more true in the relationship you have with the woman and children who trust you.

Second, verbal stabbing produces bleeding children. I'm alarmed at this form of child abuse in our country. Yes, it's child abuse when children experience the verbal explosions of their parents. A woman once said to Ron, "I hate yelling and screaming at my kids. But that's all I learned in my family—screaming and being verbally furious." Verbal stabbing produces bleeding children. You may be used to it and your children may hide from it, but as a dad and husband, as a man who wants to be a hero to his family, you must take the lead in treating the ones you love with verbal respect.

5. *The principle of financial stability.* Many men are immature in the area of finances. It often is one of those fantasy lands that many men live in, a place where they never confront reality.

One of the key concepts that many men fail to confront is the importance of beating inflation. Author Dan Benson says that if someone plans to retire in thirty years at age sixty-five with a yearly income equivalent to $45,000 in today's dollars, that person will need an annual income of $146,000 by retirement time in the year 2021. And if the person lives to be ninety, because of the effect of inflation, the income will need to rise to $389,000.

You can't ignore the eroding effects of inflation, yet many men do. What are you going to do to give your family a proper income in your later years?

Another key financial concept men fail to confront is the importance of discipline in spending. In the 1980s consumer credit doubled in this country. That's unbelievable. That's hundreds of millions of dollars. I don't mean mortgages on houses or investment property, but consumer credit—credit cards, installment debt.

Our whole society, through the media and the advertising industry, creates a societal obsession with spending. In our culture we are taught to spend money rather than save it. In the U.S. the savings rate at the end of the 1980s was hovering between 3.5

> *In our culture
> we are taught
> to spend money
> rather than
> save it.*

and 5 percent. Many people saved nothing. In Japan, the average savings rate was between 15 and 20 percent of their income. No wonder there is so much capital available in Japanese enterprise.

I read about one couple who had received a number of credit cards in the mail after they were married. As their spending habits got the better of them, they gradually fell further into debt, until they found themselves owing $32,000 on a grand total of sixty-three credit cards. Unbelievable.

Even financial counselors will tell you the two primary reasons people get credit cards are to show ID for a check and for emergencies. That's reasonable and understandable—if you are disciplined and use the credit cards only for those reasons. But what if one day you wake up and think you have a VCR emergency? Or a vacation emergency? Or a clothing emergency? It's a fake emergency—suddenly you just "have" to have something and you use your credit card. Quickly it's a financial fantasyland. So even if you say you have credit cards only for ID and emergencies, take a hard look and evaluate your "emergencies" closely.

A family built on strong financial ground is a stable family. The man who is financially responsible is a mature leader for his wife and kids.

One definition of maturity: "The ability to do a job whether or not you are supervised, to carry money without spending it, and to bear an injustice without wanting to get even."

I often speak to people who have terrible financial instability, and I give them counsel and explain how to budget and build a business. I see firsthand how important this principle of financial stability is. A family built on strong financial ground is a stable family. The man who is financially responsible is a mature leader for his wife and kids.

6. The principle of emotional availability. As we mentioned in chapter 1, so many men are present with their families in body but absent in spirit. They make themselves emotionally closed and unavailable to the people who love them.

This is what we call "life in the freezer." It's when you freeze out your wife and children. You are afraid of expressing your emotions, so you cover them up with a veneer of professionalism or aloofness or apathy.

You may not feel comfortable expressing yourself, but emotional isolation will not bring your dreams of happiness in your family to fulfillment. Life in the freezer only frustrates. It doesn't work.

Today we have the technological capacity to talk to people all over the world. We can fax, telephone, modem— all with lightning speed. Now isn't it remarkable you can communicate so skillfully all over the world, but find yourself unable to communicate with your wife in your own home?

Ron has counseled many couples over the years. He says that the number-one complaint women have in marital counseling sessions is that their husbands don't talk to them. The husband isolates himself emotionally, and communication suffers.

Earlier in my life I was intensely shy. I had trouble talking to people, but decided that for my business to grow, I needed to develop people skills. If I could do that to build my business, you certainly can do that to love your family and meet the needs of your wife and children. Reach their heart through sharing your own. Practice conversational skills. Learn the art of thought questioning. That means avoiding surface questions, such as, "How are you today?" "How's the weather?" "What's for supper?" Those are easy, cheap questions. Anybody can give a basic piece of information and satisfy the question. Thought questions—"What do you think of what the president said in his speech this week?" "How do you feel about what happened at school yesterday?" "How do you feel about our relationship as husband and wife?" "What do you want most in life?" "What dreams are coming true for you?"—are questions that open people up. It's a way for you to show your interest in significant things, and perhaps it will become a way for you to practice the principle of emotional availability.

7. The principle of natural authority. Too many men show their immaturity by forcing their authority on their families. They become iron-fisted bosses.

No doubt at these times they're in charge, but while they exercise their authority they crush the spirit of their children. They destroy the harmony of their home. They shatter the self-esteem of the woman who depends on them for emotional security and love.

Is this characteristic of you?

You have to understand that when you insist on this great

show of authority, it really is a sign of your true weakness. We're not meaning to offend you, but if you feel such a compelling need to prove your authority all the time, don't you see that indicates you are insecure about your authority? You have to prove it because you fear you don't have it.

Some men let this problem extend to the point of physical violence. We have only one thing to say to that: There is no excuse for physical violence, ever. We hope, prayerfully, that this is a problem that is not present for you. More likely your problem is that you're so insistent on your authority that you verbally pound it into your children and wife, trying to prove you're the boss. But this is damaging too.

> *You are the source for your wife, for your family— the source of financial security and emotional stability, of direction and godliness.*

Now, we believe what the Bible teaches, that the man is the head of the home and the God-appointed leader of the family. But just because you are the head of your family and leader of your home does not give you the authority to destroy the people in it. Ron tells us that in the Bible the Greek word for "head" literally means "source." You are the *source* for your wife, for your family—the source of financial security and emotional stability, of direction and godliness. Just as the head of the river is the source of the water that flows from that river into the sea, so your authority is not something you must demonstrate to prove you're the boss. If that's your pattern, that's a mark of male immaturity.

You see, your authority is naturally given, from God. You need to trust God that your natural role as leader and "source" for your family will be respected by your wife and children. Chances are, if you ease up, and not try to prove yourself so strongly, you'll find that your authority will be respected more, not less. This does not mean that you give up the leadership of your family. I know the strong feminist movement in our culture is an influence for many of you. Let me say again, I would never support harm or abuse toward wife or children. But you still must lead! Ron and I both believe that the feminist movement would not even exist if men were the strong, loving, godly leaders they are created to be. Lead with respect, lead with sensitivity, lead with love, but make sure you LEAD!

> *You see, your authority is naturally given, from God.*

8. The principle of responsibility acceptance. Men have a great capacity for making excuses for their failures. This is the final mark of immaturity that you must overcome to succeed and be a winner. And this is a big one.

Many men make too many excuses for the failures in their lives.

I recently studied a book by an author who said that every man grows up with an internal, psychological contract. For most men, that contract is with your father. This psychological contract originates in what your father, or some authority figure in your life, expects from you. If your father makes it clear that he expects you to go to college and become a professional and own your own home, then that becomes your psychological contract. You may not even be aware of it, but it's there. What happens when you fulfill the psychological contract? You stop and go into a holding pattern for the rest of your life. Think about it. Let's say you go to college and become a dentist. That's a respected profession. Now you're thirty-eight years old, established in your practice; you own your own home, and you've done everything your father expected you to do. But suddenly you find that you're beginning to coast, and you have no more dreams. Your goals are flat and empty. The zip is gone, and you just become a survivor for the next forty years.

Is that the picture of your life?

That could be an explanation as to why you have not

succeeded beyond the point where you are right now. Maybe you need to make a new psychological contract with yourself. How far do you want to go? How big do you want to dream?

> *You have potential for achieving great things for yourself and your family. But the immature man makes excuses, avoiding the responsibility of his own potential.*

How high will you reach? What does God want from you? Are you dead at thirty-eight? Done for at fifty? Or is there more for you to do, more for you to achieve in your life?

You need to accept responsibility for your failures.

You also need to accept responsibility for your potential. You have potential for achieving great things for yourself and your family. But the immature man makes excuses, avoiding the responsibility of his own potential. It's a fear of failure.

Don't let that happen to you. At home, accept responsibility for your shortcomings. Create a new contract with yourself, set new goals, and then take on the responsibility for your potential.

The average American man works 76,900 hours in his lifetime. What do you want to produce with 76,900 hours?

You don't want to get to the end of your life and look back on a trail of excuses. It would be far better for you to try and then fail miserably than to live life in the realm of excuses.

Men who become heroes to their families are men who choose to do something with all those hours. They don't allow somebody else to decide what those 76,900 hours are worth.

You must decide what they're worth because those hours are your life, your blood, your sweat, your time, your life. You need to choose. Be a man who accepts responsibility for his life.

Chapter 3

DEVELOPING A WINNING CHARACTER

Recently someone recommended a video to Ron. It was a cult film—a movie that wasn't really big at the box office, but that gathered a cult following. It's listed in most movie books as probably the worst movie ever made. It's called *The Attack of the Killer Tomatoes.* Ron didn't expect much when he rented the movie, but it proved to be even dumber than he thought it would be. It was about voracious, violent tomatoes rolling through town, squashing innocent people in their path. It wasn't horrifying—it was just plain stupid.

But when he returned the movie, he saw that the movie

had spawned successors! Not only *The Attack of the Killer Tomatoes II,* but also *The Attack of the Killer Clowns* and *The Attack of the Killer Bimbos.*

If you want to be a hero to your family, you need to overcome these character killers and stop them before they stop you.

Well, maybe that movie did accomplish one good thing. It gave us the idea for this chapter, which we've given the more dignified title of "Developing a Winning Character" but which could easily be called "The Attack of the Character Killers."

Actually, while this title might be funny, the subject matter is serious. One of the enemies of successful family life are those infiltrators that creep into your life and erode your character. They are slow, small, subtle, and sometimes silent—but they are killers.

I don't follow sports at all, but I'm told that not long ago Bart Giamatti, the baseball commissioner known for his judgments in the case of the Pete Rose scandal, suddenly died of a massive heart attack. An autopsy was performed. The coroner discovered that there had been a series of silent heart attacks that Giamatti and his family had known nothing about. There was damage that indicated the heart difficulty and showed that there had been three or four heart attacks. But Giamatti hadn't even been aware of them. They were silent heart attacks.

Character attacks can happen slowly and silently. And it can destroy you and your relationship with your wife and children. If you want to be a hero to your family, you need to overcome these character killers and stop them before they stop you.

I'd like to tell you about six character killers that I think are the most common threats to family life. See if these characteristics are part of your life, and discover how you can change yourself to overcome them.

1. Avoiding relationships. Occasionally you run across somebody who is very active in your business, your network, or your career, and who never sees his wife and children. He says it's because he is building a business. On further investigation we discover he is using success and business-building as an excuse to neglect his family. That's wrong, and its a sure prescription for failure of a marriage and home.

Yes, sometimes you have to be away from your family. But don't make the business an excuse to avoid a marriage that is not working. Instead, find out why you don't want to be with your wife. Admit to yourself that it's not the business that's taking you away from home, but it's of your own choosing.

Success is a balance. It's not just work and business and money, but also your marriage, your family, your

Success is a balance. It's not just work and business and money, but also your marriage, your family, your morals, your character, and your relationship with God.

morals, your character, and your relationship with God. Your whole life has to be in balance. It's like a symphony orchestra in which each instrument plays its proper part. The result is beautiful music. Your life should be like beautiful music. When you start avoiding relationships, using business as an excuse, your life is out of tune.

Psychologist David Elkind tells the story of when he sat in on his son's nursery school class. He was invited to observe a problem child in the class, but another experience proved to be more insightful:

> *I was sitting and observing a group of boys, including my son, who sat in a circle. . . .*
>
> *Their conversation went like this: Child A: "My daddy is a doctor and he makes a lot of money and we have a swimming pool." Child B: "My daddy is a lawyer and he flies to Washington and talks to the president." Child C: "My daddy owns a company and we have our own airplane."*

*Then my son said (with aplomb, of course):
"My daddy is here!" with a proud look in my
direction. Children regard the public presence of
their parents as a visible symbol of caring and
connectedness that is far more significant than any
material support could ever be.*

I'm not saying here that material support and financial security are not important. It's just that you must always stay clear on your motivation for work. You want to succeed to strengthen your family. Be a leader who takes care of those you love.

2. Mismanaging money. In the last chapter we talked about the area of finances being an area of immaturity for many men. This is a different problem, although it also involves money. Here we're not

> **Your whole life
> has to be in
> balance. It's like
> a symphony
> orchestra in
> which each
> instrument plays
> its proper part.
> The result is
> beautiful music.**

talking about failing to pay a bill or forgetting a bank deposit. We mean situations in which you buy something on credit when you don't have the money to cover the purchase, or when you use income in irresponsible ways when you should be paying off debt. The problem is that when you become financially dependent on bank and credit agencies, there is great pressure for you to handle financial pressures dishonestly. Whether this involves cheating on your income tax or lying about something else, it is something that erodes your character.

This is a character killer because when you mishandle money, it places great pressures on your integrity and honesty.

3. Feeding your brain junk food. Many men ingest some great business and motivation books and tapes on a regular basis, as well as various seminars, using that input to generate business ideas and new operating techniques. It's important to continuously reeducate yourself and extend your understanding into new areas.

> *Unfortunately many men also try to spice up their life with material that has no business being in their brain.*

Unfortunately many men also try to spice up their life with material that has no business being in their brain. Maybe it starts with an R-rated movie or an off-color TV show. Maybe it involves an occasional look at a pornographic magazine. Many men become gradually drawn into such things, and before they know it, those things become a regular part of their life.

Recently I came across an interesting sociological study that interviewed people who travel as part of their business.

When men, particularly, are at the end of a hard day in a strange place where no one knows them, they become vulnerable to fleshly interests. For many men it's a means of achieving a semblance of intimacy in a foreign place. Of course, using movies and books in this way is not real intimacy. It's mental junk food. And it can really damage your marriage relationship and your home life.

Here's a free tip: For as much time as you spend reading business and motivation books, consider adding to your reading list some books on marriage and relationships. Just as you need to work at keeping up in business, you need also to work to maintain and cultivate your marriage. Put *health* food into your brain, not junk food.

4. Indulging in fantasy life. It begins in your mind. You've got the key to your brain, and you unlock the power of your imagination. The imagination can be a powerful tool to build your business. You can imagine where you're going financially; you can picture financial freedom; you can envision a future of job independence.

But your mind can work the other way too. You can imagine what it would be like with the wife of the guy you just sponsored. You can imagine what it would be like if your wife wasn't around any longer. You can imagine what it would be like if you just didn't have to pay that bill or could cheat to get an extra sum of money.

Indulging in sinful fantasies makes your mind into a cesspool and damages your integrity and credibility with your wife and children.

5. Nurturing secret sins. Sin that other people can't see is a difficult thing to give up. It may be hypocrisy, greed, dishonesty, cheating, lust, sexual sin—you are the only one who really knows.

The Bible says, "Be sure your sin will find you out." You can't avoid it or escape it. Your sin will limit you, damage you, destroy you. Most important, it will take a toll on those people you love at home. What will you do to them in the effort to keep your sin a secret? What will your covering up do to your relationships?

There's a verse in Psalm 19: "Cleanse me from these hidden faults." Do you wonder why your energy is being sapped, why you're not a hero to your family? Is it possible that you have a divided heart, that you know that there are things in your private life that are wrong? Slowly, like termites, your secret sins are eating into the foundation of your house.

6. Loving something God hates. A man came to Ron recently. The man was in a bad marriage situation: he and his wife were considering divorce. He said, "Ron, I'm trying to work all this out legally, and in the meantime I'm sexually starved. Somebody told me the Bible said it was all right if I find another woman during this temporary time just for sex. Isn't it true that there's a verse in the Old Testament that says that?"

Well, after the look of horror faded from Ron's face, he replied, "The Bible says, 'You must not commit adultery,' and then it says in the New Testament that all fornication is wrong."

"What's that mean?" the man asked.

"Fornication," Ron said, "is from a Greek word that means any sexual involvement outside of marriage—period. The Bible is clear—that's wrong. It's sin."

We're still not sure where the man got his ideas about the Bible permitting sex outside of marriage, but apparently the man changed his tune and later avoided other sexual relationships.

Loving some-thing that God hates is the ultimate charac-ter killer—it literally kills your character from inside.

The point is that if you ever learn to love something God hates, you will find all kinds of ways to justify it—maybe even to the extent of using the Bible.

We believe in a real devil. Ron says that the word for "devil" in Greek means "enemy, adversary, opposer." When you love something God hates, Satan will do two things with your emotions. He will try to make you think that because you've already done something wrong, there's no hope and you might as well do it again. Satan also uses your hurt emotions or your loss of self-esteem to make you hate yourself. He hates you, and he works to get you to hate yourself.

So loving something that God hates is the ultimate character killer—it literally kills your character from inside.

There is a solution to this. Listen to the love of God.

Unfortunately, many people, men especially, neglect the spiritual dimension of their lives.

You know the familiar story; maybe it's happened to you: The family is on vacation. The man is driving. They're in a foreign city, and they're completely, hopelessly lost. Of course, the man, being proud, won't admit he's driving in circles. There's a map in the glove compartment, but he refuses to use it. *I can get my way out of this,* he thinks.

Living life without God is like driving without a map. And many men are too proud to admit they are spiritually lost.

Listen, if you spend time reviewing your marketing plan every night, and you haven't spent fifteen minutes in the Bible, you've got your priorities really out of sync. You're a victim of God-starvation.

You need to listen to the love of God, through the Bible. Don't listen to your wounded emotions, your self-hate, the devil whispering negative thoughts in your mind. Listen to the love of God.

This is the only way you can defend yourself against character killers.

> E*ven if marriages are made in heaven, man has to be responsible for the maintenance.*
>
> *Kroehler News*

Chapter 4

DEVELOPING A WINNING MARRIAGE

God wants you to have a marriage that is not only emotionally and spiritually satisfying but also physically and sexually exciting.

You've probably heard me talk about building your business and how you'll never build a big business unless you really *want* a big business. The same thing applies in marriage. You must *want* your marriage to work. The problem many men encounter is that they never invest the energy in their marriage that they invest in their business. If men wanted their marriage to succeed as much as they desire their business to succeed, we'd have a much lower divorce rate.

I am committed to Birdie; committed to our marriage for life. This commitment was made in the early years of struggle, before the money and the public attention. It began in love.

Birdie describes in her own words the tests we faced at the start.

"We lived in a $25-a-month apartment, with no heat and no hot water. We had to buy our own heater. We went to our parents' place and took a bath once a week, and between that we just washed up. But we had to heat all our water. The bathroom was down the hall, and in the winter it was real cold. We had rats in the apartment building. And since there was no heat in this apartment, in the winter the water would condense on the inside walls and would run down the walls. Of course, we had fought cockroaches since we'd lived there.

"When we had the twins, we stayed with my mother about six months until we found another place. We just let the apartment go. We all stayed in one room, the babies and us in one bedroom. So, after we moved out of there, we moved into this little house across from the dealership where Dex worked, and that was a hole in the wall, terrible. The basement was terrible. It needed a new furnace, which didn't come until winter started, so we spent that first month with his parents because it was so cold.

"Then Dex bought a trailer. I hated it. But I didn't say anything. I let him think it was OK. We had three babies by this time. It was a one-bedroom, and the toilet was terrible. It wasn't a regular flushing toilet. There was no place to wash out the dirty cloth diapers. It was very small. We lived there that winter, and then in the spring Lisa was coming. I just couldn't stay there with four babies. So it happened that some friends of ours were moving out of this house in town, and it was a big three-bedroom, so we rented the house. And that's where we lived when we started our business."

You can see some of what we battled through together. I can never repay Birdie for the loyalty she has always shown. I owe her my performance and support. I give her my love. She is the greatest motivator in my life.

Remember who you married. Remember the love and loyalty. Your marriage is worth the work that goes into it.

Ron and I would like to suggest seven simple strategies to develop a winning marriage. They're all based on that simple assumption we just talked about: That you want your marriage to succeed, and you're willing to work toward that goal.

1. Guard against unfaithfulness! Never cheat!

There is never an excuse to violate the trust one partner has in the other. There is never a good reason to violate the vows of your marriage.

Recently I finished examining a book, *Addicted to Adultery.* It's the remarkable story of Richard and Liz Brzeczek. Brzeczek was the police superintendent of the city of Chicago. At one time he was rumored to be next in line to replace William Webster as head of the FBI. He was leader of the second largest police force in the nation. He was a political power in Chicago's democratic machine. In his late thirties he became so wrapped up in his celebrity image and his power that he got cocky and became involved in a sexual relationship with an airline attendant. He said he never realized what was going to happen. He never realized that he was unleashing grave consequences. He had no idea what his fling of sinful pleasure was going to produce.

> *Unfaithfulness is not only wrong; it's stupid.*

What happened to him is an incredible story. He describes how he alienated his four children, how he devastated his believing, supporting wife, how he lost his position as police superintendent, how he lost his six-figure salary with a prestigious Chicago law firm, and how he ultimately ended up in a psychiatric hospital.

At forty years of age he was broken and defeated, wondering what had gone wrong.

He managed to pull his marriage back together, breaking off with the airline attendant. But she took him to court, and Brzeczek was indicted.

Unfaithfulness is not only wrong; it's stupid. You don't know what devastation it will do to others or yourself. Brzeczek said, "I thought of my wife. After a while I decided that I did not want a divorce. I just wanted my wife and my mistress both. I wanted to have my cake and eat it too. I never realized the destruction I was creating in my home." Of course, Brzeczek's wife went through hell. His children called his mistress one night, leaving a message on her answering machine that said, "Merry Christmas, Diane. We want to thank you for destroying our lives."

Faithfulness is the bedrock of your marriage relationship.

Brzeczek writes, "I had a wife who loved me, children who respected me, a position of influence, and I let it go down the drain because of the foolishness of unfaithfulness."

Faithfulness is the bedrock of your marriage relationship. When you become involved in adultery, you are saying more than just that you have an unfulfilled sexual need or that you are bored in your marriage. You are saying that your wife is no longer your intimate friend, your life partner, the one with whom you have a mutual trust. Unfaithfulness destroys that trust. To violate your marriage is to cut into the heart and soul of who you are as a married couple.

2. Resolve to pursue your marriage commitment.

Bill Cosby has talked about the terrible damage he did to his family when he was a young man. He went through a time when he slept with many other women. He has told how broken his wife, Camille, was about his behavior, and he said, "I realized that as I was trying to have all my fun, I was crushing the heart of my wife who loved me and trusted me. I woke up one day and said, 'I've got a commitment here, and I'm breaking it because of my own selfishness.'"

Pursuing your commitment is essential because it bases your marriage not on feelings, but on principles.

He then went to a jewelry store and bought a men's bracelet. He still wears this today. Written on it are the words: "I am Bill Cosby. I am Camille's husband." He said he wears that all the time to remind him that he's not just anybody—he's her husband, and that means everything to him. Today they have a successful marriage, but they came so close to losing it completely.

Pursuing your commitment is essential because it bases

your marriage not on feelings, but on principles. Ron was once talking to a young man who is a counselor and a pastor, and who had just counseled a couple that was heading for divorce. This couple had said, "We don't feel like we love each other any more. We want to be with somebody else." They had been married eight years. The love feelings they'd had at first had diminished, and now they wanted to move on to other relationships.

Do you see the foolishness of this couple? They thought that by moving to other relationships, they each would be happier. But they failed to understand that fulfilling relationships are based on commitment, not just feelings. Since they were not capable of commitment in their marriage, how could they achieve a successful relationship with someone else? Their inability to commit themselves to each other will haunt them from relationship to relationship.

3. Discover the power of simple human courtesy in your marriage.

It's sometimes amazing how insensitively a married couple can treat each other. Perhaps it's natural—when you live with someone for such a long while, you take things for granted, certain behaviors become routine, and you find yourself treating your partner shabbily. But a good strategy for a successful marriage involves rediscovering the basic humanity of your wife and treating her with dignity and courtesy.

Ron tells of a time when he and his wife, Amy, were shopping. Ron was frustrated because he felt she was taking too much time. He found himself rushing her along, and in the process he became irritable and treated her in a mildly rude way. He remembers how he heard himself talking to her, as if a tape recorder were playing his own words back to him. He realized he wouldn't talk to a friend or even a stranger in such a way, and how inappropriate it was for him to talk to Amy like he had. He apologized to her, asking her to forgive him. He realized that if he were to treat anyone with courtesy, it should be his wife.

Human courtesy is a crucial strategy in the battle for your marriage.

I had an experience once with a man who has his own business. This guy has people skills like you wouldn't believe. When you're doing business with him, he makes you feel like royalty. But one day his wife called him at work. When he found out it was his wife on the line he responded gruffly, "What do you want? Don't you know I'm busy? Call me later," and he hung up. I listened as this man treated his business associates like royalty but his wife like dirt.

Human courtesy is a crucial strategy in the battle for your marriage. Yes, it is challenging—it's easier to be discourteous when you know somebody so well. But, when you think about it, your wife is the one person on earth you should hold in highest esteem. Treat her well, with love and human dignity.

4. Practice daily maintenance of your marriage.

Too many couples get married and think that all the hard work—dating, courting, engagement, planning—has just ended. The truth is that it's just begun.

In manufacturing, you know the importance of maintaining machinery. In business, you know how to maintain contacts and clients in your network. Likewise, you have to maintain your marriage. We'd like to suggest four techniques for daily maintenance of your marriage:

First, spend time together. A lot of men get sidetracked by talking about quality time versus quantity time. What if you walked into the best restaurant in Washington, D.C., and you had heard that it had the most phenomenal steak dinner on the East Coast? And let's say you were drooling over this. It was $40 a person for this steak, a la carte. Salad is extra. You order. Then after a long wait, they bring out this steak and put it in front of you. Well, it's barely the size of a half dollar. You look at the steak and you say, "Where's the rest of it?" The waiter indignantly stares down and says, "But sir, it's not the quantity but the quality that counts. That's a great little piece of meat."

In your marriage you can go around saying, "I'm going to have quality time with my wife. I can fit her in here for a couple hours. Now, it may not be much time, but I'll make sure it's going to be quality time." This reveals the problem of the quality time approach: it watches the clock. It focuses on making small amounts of time into important, "quality" events. Often what is needed in a relationship is quantity time—time to relax with each other, time to experience life together, time to enjoy each other. This kind of time

> *A lot of men take charge of problems in their business, but fail to take charge of what's wrong in their marriage.*

can't be condensed and intensified to give it higher value. You need heart time with each other.

Second, talk everything out. Those words are deliberately chosen. Don't let stuff fester and sit. If there's a problem between you, discuss it. Sometimes this can be hard. You need to be open and honest with each other about everything—feelings, fears, sexual preferences, emotional needs, anger, depression, and so on. Talk it out so it doesn't blow you out. You don't want something to build up pressure in your marriage until it just explodes.

Third, if there's something wrong in your marriage, make it right—and fast! A lot of men take charge of problems in their business, but fail to take charge of what's wrong in their marriage. Solving marriage problems starts with talk, but must then progress to solid action.

Ron told me about a time when he and Amy were first married. They had a major clash about something—a full-scale argument. Amy had college classes to attend, and Ron had to go to graduate school classes. Neither of them could afford to miss any more school time and were in some hot water for that already. But they took action to resolve their conflict, and for two solid hours they talked until they worked things out. They missed their classes, but they ironed out a major conflict together. If something is wrong, get it right fast. Do what is necessary to resolve those conflicts.

Fourth, if someone needs to change, make sure you do the changing first. Men and women can get petty about personal change. "OK, I'll change if you will." "I'll change, but you go first." Men, take the initiative. Act to make changes in your character and personality first. Don't wait for your wife to make the first move.

5. Develop the art of good sex.

Too often in today's world we treat sex as if it were a science. We have how-to books and seminars and radio therapists telling us all about the best techniques for good sex. What we've lost is the sense of sex as an art form—a work-of-love-in-progress between a man and a woman in marriage.

An important strategy in your marriage is developing a great sex life. It's amazing how hard this is for some couples. Consider what the Bible—yes, the Bible!—says in Proverbs 5:18-19: "Rejoice in the wife of your youth. Let her breasts and tender embrace satisfy you. Let her love alone fill you with delight." In the original Hebrew, the love that's mentioned there means sexual love; the verse is talking about the delight of sex in marriage.

Kevin Leman wrote a book entitled *Sex Begins in the Kitchen.* Here's how he got his title. He said one night he really wanted sex with his wife, and she wasn't the least bit interested. He remembered that she had wanted him to do some kitchen cleaning that day. He had said to her, "I don't have time for kitchen cleaning. You have to do it." And then he suddenly realized that his wife was remembering the relationship moment he lost in the kitchen. He was paying for it in the bedroom. So what the title really means is very simple: It was in the kitchen that a relationship moment had been squandered.

God intends sex to be good—within the bounds of marriage.

Recently I saw a study of literature having to do with sexuality. The author of this study found it remarkable how much literature denied what God says about sex. These books and articles gave the impression that sex was somehow wrong, dirty, or unclean.

As Ron and I were discussing this issue in preparing the material for this book, we became convinced that it was essential to reeducate people about what the Bible teaches regarding good sex in

> *God intends sex to be good— within the bounds of marriage.*

marriage. And we believe that doing this will help clear away many of the barriers couples experience in their sex lives.

There are ten major obstacles to good sex. If you can overcome these barriers, then you are on your way to a vast improvement in your sexual enjoyment, involvement, and experience.

1. Physical fear. One young woman complained of pain during sex when she was first married. She dreaded sex, and it became a problem in her marriage. Her husband encouraged her to see a doctor, and she did. Two specialists later, they had all come to a unanimous conclusion: there was nothing physically wrong with the young woman. Eventually the couple sought counseling for what was becoming a major conflict in their marriage. What emerged was that this woman had grown up in a conservative religious family. Her mother had convinced her that sex would be horribly painful, and she had drilled into this girl's brain the idea that sexual intercourse was painful.

One barrier many people face is a fear of the physical. As with this young woman, this fear is usually without real medical justification. Still, the fear can be quite real.

God made sex to be a wonderful, enjoyable act shared by two people in marriage. If you are experiencing a physical barrier to that pleasure, seek medical help. If that is inconclusive, seek counseling. Don't let this barrier prevent you from a fulfilling sex life with your wife.

2. Guilt. Ron once asked a group of people in a seminar how many of them had had some experience growing up where they were taught that sex was dirty, unclean, somehow evil, or just not quite right. Almost every person in the room raised a hand. For many people the sense of guilt is a barrier to fulfilling sex.

There's another kind of guilt that many men feel. It's not that you think sex is dirty, but that you did something wrong in your past. Maybe you slept with other women before you were married; maybe your wife doesn't even know about your past. Your guilt block is always there, keeping you from being as intimate as you want to be.

We believe the greatest solution to this kind of guilt is the forgiveness of Jesus Christ. Ask his forgiveness for your past sin. Then let it go—because he's already taken care of it!

3. Ego embarrassment. Are you embarrassed that you're not able to perform the way you think you should? It may surprise you—this is a common barrier to good sex.

Maybe deep down you're afraid you can't fulfill your wife in bed; perhaps you feel expectations to be a fabulous lover. You have doubts about your ability in these areas, and so you feel inadequate in your sexuality.

Remember this—your sexuality is a logical extension of your personality. What you are as a person is who you are in sex. All you really have to do in bed is be yourself.

> *Talk with your wife about your mutual sexual needs and desires.*

What can you do about ego embarrassment? This is where sexual communication is vital. Many couples seem able to talk about everything but sex. Some have been married forty years and have had four or five children, but have never really discussed anything sexual. It may feel awkward at first, but you'll get past that stage. Make the effort to talk with your wife about your mutual sexual needs and desires.

One word of warning: make sure you're not causing

your wife some ego embarrassment by insisting she do something sexually that she doesn't want to do. This is a common pattern in men, and it causes great frustration in both a husband and wife. Sex between you and your wife needs to be mutual and loving. In order to do this, you need to communicate about sex in loving ways.

4. The elusive dream of perfect sex. In the course of married life, not all sex will be a mountaintop experience. Yet many couples expect that it should be, and they become disappointed when their sexual times together become ordinary. The dream of perfect sex inhibits their intimacy.

The lie that sex must be perfect is told to us through the media—TV, movies, books, advertising. But this isn't a real-world possibility.

Remember that the purpose of sex is the expression of love between you and your wife. It isn't a contest or a sporting event. Your worth to your wife does not depend on your ability to give her perfect sex. Her worth to you should not be based on her ability to give you perfect sex.

5. Physical inhibitors. This may sound trivial, but it's a common obstacle to a good sex life. Ron was doing a seminar on the subject of sex and marriage. He remembers that one man, when asked about all the things that can inhibit good sex in marriage, replied, "Dirt. When someone's dirty, there's body smell." In the seminar, this was a bit of an embarrassing moment, but when Ron thought about it later, he realized there was a truth in this man's comment.

Often men and women forget about those simple matters of cleanliness and hygiene that make them attractive to each other. This is just common sense. Observe personal cleanliness. Take care of yourself physically. Give your sexual life the opportunity to flourish.

6. The whipped-puppy syndrome. One of the greatest barriers to good sex in marriage is when a husband becomes subservient to his wife and begins to act like a whipped puppy. When a man begins to act like a martyr in his home, his wife loses respect for him. This destroys a couple's sex life.

We believe the Bible clearly says that the man is the head of his home. The Bible says that the husband is head of the wife as Christ is the head of the church. It doesn't mean that a man is a tyrant or a cruel monster. You see, there's a balance: The Bible also says that the man should love his wife as Jesus loves the church. If you're in proper balance in your marriage, you're going to be the right kind of leader, and you're going to love your wife. You won't allow yourself to become a whipped puppy. This doesn't mean that you can't be open to constructive criticism or that you should try to keep your wife subservient to you. After all, marriage is a partnership. Falling into the whipped-puppy syndrome destroys the mutual, sharing relationship that is essential to a good sex life.

7. The madonna-whore complex. Ron says that this is a common psychological term, and it refers to a specific pattern in male sexuality. Some men, when they marry, look at their wife as if she's a madonna, a sacred woman, like the virgin wife. And so, sexually, they treat her with too great a sense of awe, even fear. But then the man's sexual needs aren't being dealt with. He begins to seek sex elsewhere—which is why the term *whore* is used by psychologists in this phrase.

Making your wife into a madonna image isn't fair to her. She's not that, and she doesn't want that. And of course, seeking sex outside of your marriage is wrong and destructive.

How do you overcome the madonna-whore complex? If it's a serious problem in your marriage, seek counseling. Another solution might be to do some role playing with your wife. (It could be fun!) Think of your wife as your mistress. Play out the scenario. Explore a role-play scenario of hers, and maybe it will help you to think of her in more realistic (and enjoyable) terms.

In any case, don't let yourself fall victim to the madonna-whore complex. It's a serious obstacle to a good sexual relationship.

8. The incest taboo. When a husband and wife go for a long time without sex, they begin to fall into a brother-sister pattern in their relationship. At that point the taboo of incest becomes a barrier to a good sexual relationship. The husband or wife becomes disinclined to initiate sex with the other.

This is a difficult pattern to get out of once it starts, so don't let it happen in your marriage. Remember that God created sex for marriage—it is proper and right and meant to be a frequent part of the relationship between a husband and wife.

9. The grass-is-greener mentality. This is the curiosity factor—wondering what sex would be like with someone else. Would you be more sexually fulfilled with someone else? Is the grass greener with another partner?

There are several problems with the grass-is-greener mentality. First, it's based in a fantasy world. Face it, men, sex with someone else is still just sex. Sex with another person outside your marriage would not be based on love, would involve a lot of guilt, and ultimately would still just be sex—a physical experience. Second, the grass-is-greener mentality assumes that sex is what's important. It's not—love and commitment are. Third, the grass-is-greener mentality usually springs from an avoidance of dealing with problems in the marriage. Face reality: focus on those problems with your wife, and solve them. Great sex is possible within your marriage. Finding it outside your marriage is unlikely, unrealistic, and unrighteous.

10. The poison of bitterness. This is a giant sex inhibitor. When you resent one another, when there are areas in which you have not forgiven your wife, when there are wounds that have not been healed, bitterness will grow in a marriage. What a tremendous barrier to good sex.

When you allow the possibility of divorce, even to the point of only thinking the thought, you plant in your mind a seed of destruction.

The poison of bitterness—how do you deal with it? You need to talk together about the bitterness you feel. Maybe this can be done just between the two of you. Maybe you need to seek a counselor's objectivity to referee such a discussion. Ultimately, the antidote to the poison of bitterness is God's help. You need the forgiveness of Jesus Christ. When you feel this forgiveness, it's easier for you to forgive others.

The poison of bitterness inhibits good sex, a good marriage, a good relationship, and a good life.

6. Never say *divorce.*

Recently there was a remarkable survey done of couples going through the divorce process. Ninety-seven percent of the time the couple said, "We were working our problems out until one of us verbally mentioned divorce." They all admitted that just by saying the word out loud the dynamics shifted, and the marriage rapidly deteriorated from that point on.

When you allow the possibility of divorce, even to the point of only thinking the thought, you plant in your mind a seed of destruction. All marriages go through difficulties; there are always conflicts, misunderstandings, problems to work out. When divorce is an option in someone's mind, it becomes easier not to deal with those problems and avoid the conflicts.

7. Develop a spiritual relationship together.

The most important ingredient for a successful marriage is building your relationship on a spiritual foundation. So many marriages are good up to a point, but they don't share this essential ingredient of spiritual communion.

This is a point where we must be honest about our own convictions. We believe that marriage needs to be centered in faith in Jesus Christ.

You see, we don't believe Jesus was just a great religious teacher, a founder of religion. We believe he is God in human form. He took on our sins and paid the death penalty for them. He conquered death. We believe he is alive right now.

We have a faith in Jesus Christ, and he has transformed our life in miraculous ways. One of those ways has been in the area of marriage. We speak from personal experience. A marriage centered in Christ really is the ultimate relationship. In fact, a life centered in Christ is the ultimate life. We certainly respect you if you differ on this, but this is our conviction.

You can develop a winning marriage. Guard against unfaithfulness. Resolve to commit yourself to your marriage. Discover the power of human courtesy. Maintain your marriage daily. Never say *divorce.* And develop a spiritual dimension in your marriage through a relationship with Jesus Christ.

Chapter 5

STRATEGIES FOR AVOIDING UNFAITHFULNESS

We feel so strongly about this problem of marital unfaithfulness that we wanted to devote a whole chapter to it. We believe it is a considerable problem among many people we know, and it very well may be a significant problem in your life.

A Time of Moral Collapse

We live in a time of grave moral danger. Moral challenges threaten you as a person, your happiness, your success, your most vital relationships, and your family. We are living in a time of moral collapse, and we have to get refocused on moral truth.

One of the areas of moral collapse is marriage and adultery. The prevailing casual attitude toward marriage has to change. Divorce is rampant. Sex is casual and easy, despite the AIDS scare. Extramarital affairs are prevalent.

> *It was never a bad marriage that ended the marriage—it was the affair that ended the marriage.*

All of this goes against the facts. Major studies reveal that the majority of people admit to deep unhappiness in their lives. Those people say that their marriage is a battleground, a constant fight. They're always facing the tension and hostility of their home. That is totally the opposite of what God intends for your marriage. God doesn't want your marriage to be a battlefield but a paradise of fulfillment with your partner for life.

Affair is a word I don't like much because the word has a popular mystique about it: it sounds adventurous, glamorous, and wonderful. Of course that's far from the truth. Unfaithfulness is not romantic—it's hurtful, negative, and destructive. It's something that God prohibits.

People explore adultery for different reasons. First, to escape their marriage. Second, to try to stabilize their marriage. And third, to try to survive their marriage. One psychologist has said that in his counseling experience of people in adulterous situations, it was never a bad marriage that ended the marriage—it was the affair that ended the marriage. The marriage could have been improved and saved. But going outside the relationship is what broke the relationship itself.

Four Types of Adultery

Let's take a look at four different kinds of extramarital affairs. By discovering how they happen, we can more effectively fight against them.

1. The accidental affair. These are adulterous situations that occur because of "coincidence"—two people being in the wrong place at the same time.

The problem here is that most times the accidental nature of the encounter is an illusion. Accidental affairs usually happen for several reasons. First, when a relationship is not being resisted. It's one thing to say you aren't pursuing a relationship, but another thing when you don't resist it. The "accident" isn't really so accidental. Second, an accidental affair can occur because of opportunity. Maybe a man is on the road, away from his family, his wife, and he just happens to spend extra time in the lobby of the hotel, or in a bar, or walking around the town at night. The man might protest that he was never looking to start an affair, but he put himself in situations where the opportunity presented itself. Again, the "accident" isn't really so accidental. Third, many extramarital involvements get started in the context of casual counseling situations, intimate friendships between men and women that start out innocently but turn into something dangerous. In a situation where intimate matters are being shared between a man and woman, the chances are great that a romantic relationship will begin.

2. The romantic affair. In the accidental affair, a man may wake up one day and say, "What a stupid thing I've done. I've endangered my whole marriage. I don't want this. This is wrong." But in the romantic affair, the crazy romantic begins to spin in circles of fantasy and excitement. He thinks the affair is real love when it's really just a feeling of being *in love.* He fails to see the difference.

Romantic people tend to do things because it *feels* like the right thing to do and not because it *is* the right thing to do. There are a lot of things that feel right but are hopelessly wrong. The Bible says, "Before every man there lies a wide and pleasant road he thinks is right, but it ends in death."

Don't do it. The hopeless romantic is a man or a woman who is controlled by emotions. The romantic is especially susceptible to the media: TV, movies, books, and magazines that show idealistic images of people in love.

Keep in mind that real love is developed over time, through hard work, and by virtue of two people experiencing each other over a period of time. That's why marriage is so beautiful. It's not just two people being in love, but two people who know each other deeply and love the other fully.

3. The philandering affair. This type of unfaithfulness is conducted by the man or woman who has an addiction to sexual relationships. This affair tends to be brief and intense and is followed up by another affair much like it. We know now that John Kennedy was like that. He was a strong leader, but he was a moral weakling in his private life. He experienced great loneliness in his marriage because of his philandering patterns with so many women.

It's one thing to say you aren't pursuing a relationship, but another thing when you don't resist it.

The philanderer usually has a great fear of women, or else great anger—he wants to control and possess them. He doesn't have the maturity or strength to build one relationship with one woman for life.

I believe the greatest example of manhood in this generation is staying with one woman for a lifetime. It takes a man to do that. It doesn't take a man to give up and seek other women if there's trouble in his marriage.

4. The marital arrangement. This is the situation where a man and woman are legally married, but they make an arrangement with one another, supposedly allowing each partner to have sex with other people, usually on the condition that the other partner doesn't have to know about it. This, of course, is a complete perversion of God's intention for marriage. It's destructive to all people involved. It represents a severe moral and spiritual breakdown.

Reasons for Marital Breakdown

What makes a marriage prone to a breakdown? There are five big reasons why marriages break down and affairs occur.

1. Emotional vampirism. The vampire in literature is the most selfish of all monsters. The vampire exists in loneliness and darkness, its sole purpose to suck life from the living to sustain its own life. It is always taking—never giving.

In a marriage, the emotional vampire is the partner that sucks the joy and life out of the relationship. The emotional vampire refuses to be satisfied and is always reaching for something more. He is always giving a negative broadcast in the relationship, communicating his dissatisfaction to his wife. The emotional vampire draws self-esteem out of his partner.

In time, the emotional vampire needs more and goes outside of the marriage for new victims. Ironically, his wife may also seek extramarital relief from the constant life-draining pattern of the marriage.

2. Verbal negativism. Ron was talking with a woman recently, and she was verbally criticizing her husband. That was bad enough, except that her husband was also standing right there. She was pointing out to Ron all the failures of her husband.

Don't do that to your marriage partner—either in public or in private. If you do, two things will happen. Soon you'll start to believe the bad things you're saying. You'll look beyond your wife to someone else who appears to be more perfect. And your wife will likely seek her self-esteem elsewhere.

> *In a marriage, the emotional vampire is the partner that sucks the joy and life out of the relationship.*

3. Intimacy erosion. Intimacy in marriage is eroded by dishonesty. Whenever you're not totally honest in your relationship with your marriage partner, the marriage will start to break down. It's a breaking of trust.

Are you keeping secrets from your wife or your husband? Do you realize that any time you share secrets with another person, you are creating a bond between you? Are you sharing secrets with another woman?

Dr. Frank Pitman, a psychiatrist in Atlanta, says that people come to him in his practice and say, "Well, our marriage broke up because we just grew apart."

You know what that implies—that you can't help it.

Pitman says to these people, "The truth is you didn't break up because you grew apart. You broke up because you started lying to each other, you started manipulating each other, you chose to stop communicating, and you chose to communicate confusingly when you did communicate, you chose to spend time apart too much, and you chose to move apart. You didn't break up because you grew apart. You grew apart because you chose to do things you shouldn't have done.

Intimacy in marriage is eroded by dishonesty.

Intimacy is also eroded by the failure of friendship. Statistics show that the main reason people seek extramarital affairs is friendship. Maybe they need conversation, somebody to listen to them. The average couple in this country is estimated to spend an average of just twenty-eight minutes *a week* in intimate, close, personal conversation. Some studies of divorce have discovered that a couple does their greatest amount of talking at two points in a relationship: on the third date and a year before they get a divorce, presumably because they're fighting so much. What happened to the commitment to communicate, to be close to each other, and communicate heart feelings? Quite simply, it's a failure of friendship.

4. Sexual curiosity. As you'd expect, many people are attracted to adultery because of sexual curiosity. They wonder if sex is better with someone else. Statistics show that it isn't. More than 80 percent of those interviewed who have had sexual affairs admit that the sex itself was really a disappointment.

There was a remarkable interview in the June, 1989, *Esquire,* with funnyman Robin Williams. He was asked, "Have you ever had a mid-life crisis?" Williams replied, "I've been in one for five or six years." This time he wasn't joking. He said, "I've tried everything—the drugs, the sex with a lot of people. I've tried sports sex. I've done that, thank you. That was nuts. It was the total opposite of intimacy."

> *Marriages also break down because of spiritual emptiness in the relationship.*

That's the sexual surprise you get when you leave a marriage. The sex that you thought was going to mean so much and bring you youth and vitality ends up being a great disappointment.

5. *Spiritual emptiness.* Marriages also break down because of spiritual emptiness in the relationship. There is no loneliness like spiritual loneliness. Why? Because you were created to know God, to have a relationship with him through Jesus Christ. When you don't have that relationship, you are running on empty. And in marriage, even when the emotional

and sexual aspects of the relationship are good, there can be great dissatisfaction because of a spiritual vacuum at the core.

Affair-Proofing Your Marriage

There are ways you can specifically guard against unfaithfulness. We'd like to offer this list of seven things you can do to affair-proof your marriage:

1. Learn to face the facts about adultery. Be honest. Don't ever fool yourself. It can happen to you. Don't take your marriage for granted. One psychiatrist has said that you must realize the facts about affairs—they are not normal human behavior. They never result in happiness.

Know the facts.

Face the facts.

2. Always discuss everything in your marriage with your partner. Ron speaks honestly about his own marriage: "If I am ever in a weak, vulnerable moment or have an unusual attraction to another woman, Amy Ball is the first person to hear about it. I go to her immediately. If I'm not around her, I call her on the phone. I discuss it with her because I don't want to fight that crazy battle alone. It bonds me to Amy."

Discuss everything—even sexual temptation—with your wife.

3. Spend a lot of good time together. I well know the

pressures of time in a competitive business environment, but I maintain that if a person's time management does not include time for God and family, then something is terribly wrong.

It is astounding the number of women and men who never have an intimate time together for one evening or one day. No wonder so many marriages drift apart.

4. Manage your environment. You know about the sexual temptation of travel. When you go into a hotel alone, pray for strength to withstand the pressures of being alone. The temptations are great. Manage your environment. Ask the front desk to disconnect the Spectravision

> **When you go into a hotel alone, pray for strength to withstand the pressures of being alone.**

from your hotel room TV. Avoid eating out in bars or in places where by being alone you are vulnerable. Be careful about your physical interactions with female coworkers.

The story is told of Billy Graham, who was in a hotel room in New York City for his great 1957 Madison Square Garden Crusade. He became so absorbed in the room TV, which was a relatively new development at that time, that he was distracted from doing his spiritual preparation for the meetings. Graham reached over, took the cables, put his foot against the wall, and ripped them out, plaster and everything. He called the front desk and told them to bill him for the damage when he checked out.

That's the kind of resolve you need to manage your environment against temptation.

Let me tell you what my policy is. I never travel about with women. I guard myself so no open door to temptation even tricks me to sin.

5. *Fill up your time with positive reading and positive work.* You need to get so busy building your business, helping people, praying, reading, and studying that you don't have time to give in to temptation. Fill your time with positive, productive activities.

6. *Work hard at having good sex at home.* A good marriage has good sex. And listen, good sex gets better with practice. If this sounds like fun to you—it is! And this is the wonderful freedom of a God-ordained marriage.

However, for various reasons, not all married people find sex so easy or so enjoyable. If this is your situation, then seek some marital counseling to explore the situation. Strange things happen to married people when they don't have sex. As I mentioned earlier, if a husband and wife go long enough without having sex, they start feeling more like brother and sister. And the incest taboo will start to work psychologically, even though they're married. They find it harder to have sex the longer they don't have it.

7. Develop an abundant relationship with Jesus Christ. Just as one of the signs of marital breakdown is spiritual emptiness, so you need to fill the vacuum with a relationship to Jesus Christ. Let him fill your life, and your marriage, with spiritual joy and fulfillment. A marriage built on a relationship to Christ is the way life was intended to be, the way God designed it.

Discover the great joy that lies in that relationship.

Chapter 6

BECOMING AN EFFECTIVE FATHER

There is no subject of greater importance when you are building a family than your attitude toward your own children.

Recently Ron was speaking with a pastor friend in Kentucky. This man told Ron of two funerals he had done in recent years of two young men, both from the same family. They had a father who had known a measure of financial success, who was a professional that had been well respected in his field—and who was an alcoholic. Despite this father's success, his drinking problem had created a tremendous barrier between him and his two sons. When Ron was in this father's office recently, he noticed that he still has photographs on his wall of his sons as babies. As Ron was sitting there speaking with this gentleman, he noticed his affectionate glance every now and then toward the wall. He would look longingly toward the two young men, who were now dead. He still remained a father in his heart toward his children, and yet, with his difficulties with alcohol, his lack of discipline, and his personal irresponsibility, he had severely damaged his children.

> *There is no greater responsibility, no greater privilege, no greater opportunity for building your life into the life of other people than with the rearing of your children.*

There is no greater responsibility, no greater privilege, no greater opportunity for building your life into the life of other people than with the rearing of your children.

Recently Ron and his family were moving into a new house. He tells of the experience he had one night:

> *We had been getting the house ready to move into it. It wasn't totally ready yet, but we were all exhausted, and we decided to spend the night there.*

We threw ourselves into the one bed that we had set up. There were five of us in that one little bed—me, my wife, Amy, Allison, Allison's dog, and a stuffed animal of Allison's. So we all crowded into the bed. I remember waking up in the middle of the night with Allison's feet in my face and her dog stretched across my knees. I couldn't move. I turned and started to move the dog. Well, this dog, which I had bought for my daughter, growled at me. I very cautiously shifted the dog to another part of the bed so I could sleep. Then I began to turn Allison, whose feet were now in my stomach. So I gently moved her, and in her sleep she swung her fist in my face. I slowly moved her fist from my face, and by this time I looked over to see if I was going to get any help at all from Amy, but, of course, she was sound asleep, not moving an inch. And so I realized I had to take care of this situation all by myself. I began to move Allison again, and she flipped and flopped, and it started her dog growling again. Well, finally, around 3:00 A.M. I got everybody situated so that I could sleep through the rest of the night.

The punch line of my story perhaps is not what you expected. It wasn't what I expected. I turned and looked at Allison. I saw this sweet, seven-year-old face, and she looked so innocent and full of promise. I realized again, even after the inconvenience of the night and all my tiredness, how much love I have for Allison. It is unexplainable in human terms. I cannot find adequate words to express the emotion, the power of love I feel for my daughter, and my feelings were most powerful that night.

I want the best for her. I want to rear her in the right way. I want her to learn all the principles of success and hard work that I have learned. I want her to be ambitious. I want her to be pure and sweet. I want Allison to grow up and be the best she can be for God himself.

Now, contrast Ron's story with the account of the alcoholic man who had lost his two sons. What makes the difference between families? What's the difference between successful parents and parents who have become failures?

I have always tried to give my whole commitment to my seven children. I pray for them. I help them grow. This commitment to them is powerful in my life.

But I know that as much as you love your family, love won't be enough. It is not enough in countless families all over the world. Sometimes kids still go wrong. The road to producing mature children is filled with peril, and there are many pitfalls. James Dobson wrote a book called *Parenting Is Not for Cowards*. Yes, it takes strength and fortitude. Sometimes you do a great job and you feel terrific, other times you blow it and feel horrible.

You need some direction for rearing your children.

In this chapter we'd like to give you a road map for rearing your kids. It won't answer all your questions or solve all your problems, but it may keep you from getting lost. Perhaps it'll get you going on the right path.

> *Sometimes you do a great job and you feel terrific, other times you blow it and feel horrible.*

In the next few pages, we want to take a hard look at seven different kinds of parenting types. You may not fall into just one type: your parenting style may be different at different times. The important thing is that you identify your parenting styles and pay attention to the effect your styles have on children.

The Stern Parent

Charles Swindoll, a pastor and Bible teacher in California, once told the story of how a number of years ago he overheard his children talking. They were commenting on how their dad never laughed. "Dad is always so serious about everything. He never has fun with us, he never laughs." This really got to him. He prayed about it: "God, what's the future going to be for me? Am I going to be so stern and strict and serious that I create stress for my kids?" Hearing his kids talk about him led him to think differently about his parenting style.

The stern parent may be like a drill sergeant: orders are given, kids are expected to shape up or ship out. It's hard to believe that in this permissive age the stern parent style exists, but in fact it does.

There seem to be two basic reasons why most parents are overbearing and too strict with their kids. The first is guilt. As a parent you feel guilt about your failures and shortcomings, and you're trying to make absolutely certain that your kids don't duplicate some of your mistakes. Because of that, you crack down too much. Maybe you remember errors you committed as a kid, and you blew it at certain points. Maybe you were sexually loose and immoral when you were a teenager, and now you say, "I'm going to crack down on my kids. I'm going to make sure they don't make the mistakes I made."

The second reason parents become overbearing with their kids is that often parents have feelings of inadequacy and inferiority in their own life. Maybe you have such a strong sense of your own inadequacy that you try to make up for it by overdoing it. When you don't know how to be a good parent, when you feel that you don't have the right answers or skills, sometimes, rather than admitting that you just need help, you'll come on too strong with your kids or force your authority down their throat.

Don't let your guilt or inadequacy cause you to create greater pressure on your children.

We feel it's important to say at this point that we believe in rules and discipline. As in most things, there is a balance. As parents, you should not swing to the other extreme of permissiveness, such as occurred a generation ago. Kids require appropriate boundaries. Appropriate discipline is necessary for children.

But don't let your guilt or inadequacy cause you to create greater pressure on your children. Learn to let your guilt feelings out in the open. Admit your inadequacies. Discuss these concerns with your wife. Together create a plan for parenting your children with the right mix of discipline and freedom.

The Slick Parent

This parenting type is like what you see on sitcoms on TV. These moms and dads seem to do everything so perfectly, and they just ease in and ease out of life, seeming to have a thirty-minute answer for every problem that comes up in their TV family. They're slick.

It's impossible to achieve this in real life, of course, but some parents try to, and they manage to arrive at an easy slickness in their parenting style.

Children of slick parents tend to be driven, and seem to be endlessly chasing new achievements.

One characteristic of the slick parent is perfectionism. The slick parent expects everything to happen properly, on time, and smoothly. The slick parent imposes this perfectionism on his children, expecting them to contribute to the smooth pattern of family life. This parent tends to manipulate his children to achieve a quality end result. That manipulation values the end achievement more than the child and will be deeply resented by a child later in life.

You've probably heard that tongue-in-cheek definition of a perfectionist: One who takes pains to make sure everything is right, and then gives those pains to everybody else.

Unfortunately, this isn't so funny when it really happens in the home. In counseling one meets grown adults who are so battered with perfectionism from their slick parents that they are crippled emotionally. It's almost as if these parents were holding their children in front of the world, showing them off like status symbols, like a perfect lawn or a new car. Again, it's a way that parents compensate for their own early childhood shortcomings. It's as if they're saying to the world, "See, I wasn't such a jerk. I wasn't such a nerd. I wasn't such a fool. Look at my kids—they're great, they're perfect." Their kids are like trophies, trophies they never got earlier in life.

The slick parent creates great stress in his children. The child can grow up feeling inadequate, unable to accomplish anything worthwhile. Children of slick parents tend to be driven, and seem to be endlessly chasing new achievements. You see, the tragedy is that the child feels as if he has no personal worth apart from achieving a level of perfection. It becomes an endless cycle that haunts him as an adult.

Dr. David Elkind is the author of *The Hurried Child* and *All Grown Up and No Place to Go.* He's an author who doesn't seem to share all of our Christian principles, but he's a solid writer who has contributed good information in these areas. Elkind writes that stress in children is the number-one health care problem of this decade. Children are being stressed out because so many parents are imposing perfection upon them.

The Sloppy Parent

The sloppy parent is lazy and inconsistent. The sloppy parent is too lazy to discipline his children, and therefore is inconsistent in his approach to parenting. When kids disobey, sometimes they're punished, and sometimes they're not. It's sloppy parenting.

> *You need to make your kids a priority in your life, and devote new energy and time to these relationships.*

This type of parent is not necessarily lazy in the rest of his life. In fact, he may be a motivated, achieving person in the work world. But when he comes home, he is too tired to spend time with his children.

Now we know that you probably work very hard and that coming home after a hard day to deal with a houseful of kids is a difficult thing to do sometimes. But take our advice: You're only with your children a short time in this life. They'll grow up very fast, and before you know it, they'll be leaving home. You may have a relationship with them when they're adults, but it will probably be only as good as your relationship is with them now. Don't lose the opportunity you have with your children.

If your parenting style is that of the sloppy parent, you

may have proven that you have the biological ability to father a child and to provide your kid the basic necessities of life, but you haven't proven your ability to be a good father to your child as he or she is growing up. You are not building quality into your relationship with your child.

You need to think of your kids more often, consider their uniqueness, their worth, their need. You need to make your kids a priority in your life, and devote new energy and time to these relationships. It's the most important thing you'll ever do.

The Silent Parent

The silent parent avoids emotional involvement with his children.

Maybe as a father you have problems in this area because you grew up with the mistaken idea that being quiet and hiding your emotions and squelching your feelings was the right way to be a man. But I hope you've heard enough and read enough of the material that has come out recently that shows the faultiness of that thinking.

We believe in the principle of men being the head of the home because the Bible teaches it; it's what God says is the right order of authority in the home. But it does not mean that you can emotionally isolate yourself from your children. If you're a silent parent, then you're creating a huge emotional gulf between you and your children. It may not be something you can change or correct later on.

> *The father who is emotionally distant can affect his children in the same way as if he were not even there.*

The father who is emotionally distant can affect his children in the same way as if he were not even there. There are more than 5 million fatherless children in this country, but that doesn't include the many fathers who are physically present, but emotionally absent. To a child, it's essentially the same thing.

You need to be emotionally involved with your children. You need to get excited with them, laugh with them, relate to their hurts and tears. You need to be close to them, not only physically but also emotionally, so that they hear your love and feeling for them in the tone of your voice.

The Stupid Parent

We don't mean this parenting type to offend, but to illustrate a point. Many parents assume that parenting skills come naturally. They never consider parenting to be something that they need to learn and study.

You have probably read many books on business and

motivation to build your business. You consider your knowledge of business to be something that you've cultivated and studied. But if you approach your business this way, why not the more important task of parenting?

There are many stupid parents in the world—not because they were born stupid, but because they've chosen not to educate themselves in the skills of parenting.

Why don't we study parenting as we study other fields of endeavor?

It's not because there is a lack of opportunity. There are many books on parenting. There are parenting seminars and groups. Many churches feature study series on the subject.

> *Don't be ignorant, ill-informed, or uninformed. Do what it takes to learn what it takes to grow great children.*

So my advice is this: Learn all that you can. Don't be a stupid parent, don't be ignorant, ill-informed, or uninformed. Do what it takes to learn what it takes to grow great children.

The Sick Parent

Some parents are really sick in emotional, mental ways. Remember the man I mentioned earlier in this book, who has been so in bondage to alcoholism for years that he has virtually ruined his children? He was a sick parent. Some parents wrestle with depression and emotional problems so much that they have no capacity for parenting their children in a healthy, wholesome way. Other parents are overly possessive. I heard of a woman who was so controlling that her children finally rebelled and ran away from home. And there are, unfortunately, parents who are abusive, physically or emotionally.

Does this parenting type fit you? Maybe you were mistreated or abused as a child. Maybe you were sexually assaulted and emotionally destroyed. Maybe you grew up in a family where your father or your mother was one of these parenting types—stern, slick, sloppy, silent, stupid, sick— and it hurt you growing up.

If this description fits you, we have several suggestions.

Seek help from a professional Christian counselor. You may be hesitant to do this. You may think that counseling is for people who have "real" problems. Well, you *do* have a real problem. And besides, counseling no longer has a stigma attached to it. Many people seek counseling for a variety of needs.

If you're a sick parent, you need professional help. Make an appointment with a qualified counselor today.

Seek the assistance of your wife. Confess your need to the one you are closest to—your wife. This may be hard for you. Many men find that admitting failure is a sign of weakness. Quite the contrary, it's a sign of strength.

Your wife can help you face your problem. In fact, doing this may enhance your marriage relationship.

Read and study—about the kind of problem you have. Many sick parents also share the characteristics of stupid parents—they are woefully ignorant of their own need.

Read books that talk about the pattern of abuse, codependence, or depression—whatever problem it

Perhaps you've shut God out of your life recently. Maybe you need to approach him in prayer with your problem.

is that you face. Knowing more about your problem will help you deal with it more effectively. It will also help you discover that you're not alone. Other men face the same problems.

Seek help from God. Prayer is not a weak, sentimental activity. It is the act of connecting with the almighty God. It's tapping into divine power. Perhaps you've shut God out of your life recently. Maybe you need to approach him in prayer with your problem. Ask him to help you overcome your parental shortcomings. He will.

The Successful Parent

Yes, there are successful parents. And that really is what you want to be.

There's a great verse in the Bible about being a successful parent. It's found in the Old Testament, which is, of course, the common heritage of Christians and Jews. It's in Deuteronomy 6:4-9:

*O Israel, listen: Jehovah is our God, Jehovah
alone. You must love him will all your heart, soul,
and might. And you must think constantly about
these commandments I am giving you today. You
must teach them to your children and talk about
them when you are at home or out for a walk; at
bedtime and the first thing in the morning. Tie them
on your finger, wear them on your forehead, and
write them on the doorposts of your house!*

We want you to notice that the most powerful element of those verses is the life-style element. The verse says that it's not enough to teach the love of God, but it's important to live that teaching. This is an important principle. *The successful parent is one who practices what he teaches.*

As early as my kids could handle it, I put them to work. I decided to back up my personal work example with their own experiences. One of my son Jeff's first jobs was cleaning up at some of my construction sites. Steve remembers one summer stripping floors and refinishing a barn.

Doyle had to put in the effort to make the money. When he was old enough, I gave him a car. Not a new car, but an old one. What I called "basic transportation." He had to fix it and take care of it. It was his responsibility.

It was never enough for my kids to learn work theory; I wanted them to know work *reality.* I knew that for Dexter Jr., Doyle, April, Lisa, Jeff, Steve, and Leanne, example and experience were crucial.

> *It was never enough for my kids to learn work theory; I wanted them to know work reality.*

The Bible also says that you should talk about these principles all the time—talk about them when you get up, when you lie down—all the time. This is the principle of consistency. *The successful parent is a consistent parent.* Teaching the love of God must occur all the time, not just occasionally.

I was reading an interview with George Bush, conducted some years ago before he became president. The interviewer said, "Mr. Bush, you've had great accomplishments in your life. You built an oil company in Texas from the ground up, you've been a successful businessman. You were successful in two terms in Congress. You were successful as ambassador to the United Nations. You were successful as chairman of the National Republican party. You were special envoy to mainland China. You became vice president of the United States. And now, sir, of all these accomplishments, what are you the proudest of?"

Bush answered, "I am proudest of the fact that our children still want to come home."

Now that's what a successful parent produces: A nurturing climate, a home atmosphere where kids grow and thrive.

Gordon MacDonald, in his book *The Effective Father,* writes,

> *The challenge is in saturating the routine of normal living with the plan and the presence of God. In short, ensure that life within your home is so positive, so appealing, so fulfilling that all else in the outside world pales in contrast to what a child receives when he's with the family.*

Isn't that powerful! That's the kind of home you want. That's the type of family atmosphere you want to produce so that your kids will enjoy being with you. Not only will they want to be with you, but they'll actually be in business with you—they'll be a part of you!

> The best gift a father can give to his son is the gift of himself—his time.
>
> C. Neil Strait

Chapter 7

STRATEGIES FOR HUGGING YOUR KIDS

Becoming an effective father requires more than simply determining your parenting type.

Author Ken Canfield, in his new book *The Seven Secrets of Effective Fathers,* writes about "father substitutes"—the forces of our culture that try to take over your role in the family:

> *The TV father. Television says, "I'll watch over your children for you. I'll keep them preoccupied while you do your work and live your life." Of course, not only is the TV father notorious for*

feeding your children huge portions of the wrong foods, but it is also quite hard of hearing. There will be times your kids will want and need to express what they're thinking, feeling, and imagining, but the TV father won't listen and can't respond.

The public schoolteacher father. At some point during your children's education you can be sure there will be a public schoolteacher who will say, "I'm qualified with degrees in biology and psychology. I should be the one to teach your children about sex." Of course, the schoolteacher father is not allowed to discuss sex in a context of love or marriage.

The federal government father. Uncle Sam says to many dads, "I've got you covered. I can make sure your kids get enough to eat. I might even foot their college bill. You don't have to worry about that." This sounds too good to be true, and it is. Millions of children are supported by the federal government father while their natural father remains out of work, distant, and perhaps even absent.

You see, the stakes are high. This really is a war for the spirit of your child. You are called to be a hero and to wage war against these invading forces.

The spirit of your child is the essence of who he or she really is. If you're going to be a smart, successful parent, then you must be alert to what your children are watching on TV, know what your children are reading, be attentive to what they're learning in school. Take the time and make the commitment to actually be involved in their education. Keep in touch with their circles of friends. Fight the battle for your child's spirit.

As my kids grew up, their friends were always over. We would talk and have fun. I would challenge them to races or arm-wrestling contests. I got to know them and kept some influence over those who were an influence on my children.

I would like to tell you some of my battlefield strategies for winning the war—specifically, strategies for hugging your kids. Now these are not literally methods for hugging your children, but tips for understanding and dealing with your children in love and discipline.

The Invisible Contract

There is an emotional contract between children and parents. It's a natural, invisible contract, an assumed agreement in which the child expects certain things from you as a parent and you expect certain things from your child. It basically is an attitude of fairness between a parent and a child.

The invisible contract is invoked frequently—maybe many

times in a single day. The parent says to the child, "If you do this, then I will do this." "If you eat your carrots, then you can have ice cream." "Only when you finish your homework can you watch your favorite TV show." Sometimes the child invokes the contract: "If I mow the lawn, Dad, can I have the car tonight?"

Actually, children understand the invisible contract better than adults do. Children are super sensitive to fairness. They're not always right in their estimate of what is fair and what's not, and sometimes you as a parent have responsibilities that don't seem fair to a child but are part of the bigger world that a child doesn't understand yet. But basically, children are alert to the concept of fairness or the lack of it.

Child psychologists are just now understanding what this concept really means. Parents need to understand the invisible contract in order to understand their children effectively. If you want to be a smart, successful parent, then you need to under-

> *If you're going to be a smart, successful parent, then you must be alert to what your children are watching on TV, know what your children are reading, be attentive to what they're learning in school.*

stand the concept of the invisible contract.

The problem with the invisible contract occurs when it is violated by one or both parties. In *The Seven Secrets of Effective Fathers,* Ken Canfield writes about a personal experience with his son Joel:

> *He hears the commitments I make (both implicit and explicit) and holds me to them. For example, one day I called him from work and told him that when I got home, he and I would play catch. When I did get home, we did go outside, but instead of catch, I organized a game of kickball so that other kids, including the neighbors, could play. But Joel was disappointed. I had made a specific commitment (I had said "catch" and "he and I"), but I hadn't followed through.*

If you want to be a smart, successful parent, then you need to understand the concept of the invisible contract.

Contract violations frequently happen when the child enters the teenage years, and you don't live up to your end of the bargain. The child is getting older, gaining more responsibilities, but senses that you aren't giving him a fair portion of freedom.

As a parent, it's easy to violate the contract in your child's adolescent years. You can be understandably scared that your kids are going to turn out wrong or rebel, and you try to control them to ensure that they won't. But in fact one of the best ways to make them rebel is to apply this control upon them. You violate the contract.

> *As a parent, it's easy to violate the contract in your child's adolescent years.*

Violating the contract can create deep resentment within a child. Ron tells about an experience with his daughter, Allison, in which he forgot to do something that he had promised her:

> *I had made a human mistake: I forgot to do something for her. It was unfair to her, and I could see the resentment in Allison's eyes and in the clench of her jaw. There's nothing more devastating than looking at your daughter and seeing how badly you've disappointed her.*

You ought to be careful not to break your word with your children. Sometimes circumstances will arise when it will require your doing something that you didn't plan on; you'll have to explain to your children and they'll have to be able to handle it and understand it as best they can.

But to win the battle for your child's spirit you need to avoid a pattern of unfairness. You need to honor the invisible contract.

The Difference Between Your Feelings and Your Child's Feelings

Dr. David Elkind's research shows that a child experiences adult feelings, but has childlike thoughts.

Just because a child is young doesn't mean he or she cannot be deeply hurt. Children have emotions similar to an adults. They feel grief and anger and pain and love and excitement. They feel disappointment and anticipation, apprehension and fear, drama, excitement, and power. But they do not think the way you think. They do not have the different levels of adult thought. They do not put it together the way you put it together.

Ron tells a story about his daughter, Allison, that illustrates the truth of Elkind's finding:

Allison has always been very aggressive and rarely expresses fear. Recently we bought a house three minutes away from my mom and dad's house in my hometown in Kentucky. We were standing in the den, putting up some curtains. I said, "Allison, why don't you walk down to Nanny's house?"

Allison replied forcefully. "No!"

"Allison," I said, "you told all your friends last week that you were excited to buy the new house and live there because you could walk to Nanny's."

"No," she said, "I don't want to go. I want you to drive me."

I said, "Allison, it's in the middle of the day. All you do is walk down the back alley, there are no cars—no traffic—it goes right to Nanny's house." At this point, I probably became too much of the stern father, but I said, "Allison, you're not afraid. I haven't taught you to be afraid. Now, you walk down to Nanny's right now."

Allison clenched her fists and began to cry. "No, Daddy, no."

I told her I didn't understand. Was she afraid of something? And the moment I said the word afraid, it triggered something in her.

She said, "Yes, Daddy. I'm afraid. The man."

"What man?"

"I was walking with Nanny, and a man whistled at Nanny and asked her to stop. And Nanny wouldn't stop, and he went on, and I'm afraid that man is out there and is going to get me."

Now we live in a real tiny town where everybody knows everybody, and I'm inclined to think

*there was no real danger, but to Allison it was a
threatening situation.*

*She had felt the emotion of fear just as an
adult would, but she didn't have all the knowledge
that an adult has to deal with her fear. She didn't
think like I did: This is a small town, I know
everybody. It's in the middle of the day. I can walk
there safely. She didn't think in those terms and
wasn't able to reason it out. She just felt the emotion of fear.*

If your children do not respond the way you expect them
to respond in certain situations, it may be because they are
reacting to an emotion and don't have the rational ability to
deal with it effectively. That's why you're there. You can help
them understand various situations, and by doing so, succeed
in relieving their adult emotions.

The Difference between Attitude
and Performance

If you're an effective father, you will try to help your children
develop an attitude, a positive approach to life, an effective
way to interpret the world.

The problem many parents face is that they value
performance over attitude. It's easy for those of us who are

goal-oriented to do this. We judge ourselves by our performance in our business, and we tend to apply those values to our children.

But it's destructive to children when they sense that what's important to you is how well they do a job—their performance. If you recall, this is the pattern of the slick parent—the perfectionist—but it's a trap that all parents can fall into from time to time.

> *It's destructive to children when they sense that what's important to you is how well they do a job—their performance.*

When a child feels as if his worth depends on his performance, he can become paralyzed with fear, performance-anxiety, and start to get down on himself.

Instead, you need to emphasize attitude over performance. What matters is not whether your child hit a home run, but how hard he or she tried in the batter's box. It's the effort, the attitude, that should matter. Now if your child *does* hit a home run—of course, reward the performance. But make sure your child understands that he or she would have been just as loved if the result had been a strikeout.

The Value of Your Own Childhood Memories

It's been a long time since you were a child, and you may have lost touch with what it was like. A very helpful exercise is to travel back to those days and put yourself in a child's shoes once again.

Ron recalls an experience of his childhood that has proven helpful to him in understanding his daughter's feelings:

When I was ten years old, my family moved to Huntington, West Virginia. It was a traumatic and difficult experience for me. When I went there, I made only a few friends. As time went on, I adjusted and eventually came to like Huntington a great deal. But within the first several months, I got in trouble at school.

It had never happened before and never since, but it did happen this one time.

I was walking with a friend of mine down the hallway. He was a rebellious kid and was always in trouble, but he was likable in a daring sort of way. I enjoyed being with him.

One time in school he said to me, "Ron, why don't you go home with me?"

"I can't go home with you," I said, "we're in school."

"No, the teachers let me go home all the time. My mother is there, and I have special permission from the school to go home."

Somehow I believed him and agreed to leave school with him. So we walked the six blocks from the school to his house. At the front doorstep, he pulled a house key from under the mat. Inside, we drank Cokes and ate potato chips.

I began to realize that there was no mom there. Soon we walked back to the school grounds. We had been gone for over an hour. Something inside told me, "This doesn't feel right."

As we walked into the school building an irate, angry teacher turned the corner, grabbed us, and yelled, "Where have you been?" She took us to the principal's office.

All the while I was thinking, Hey, this teacher is just ignorant. She doesn't know about the special permission. We'll inform her. "Hey, there's no problem," I said. "Ask my friend here. We had special permission to go to his house. He does this all the time." I turned, grinning to my friend.

But he shook his head and said to the teacher, "Ron made me do it. I didn't want to go."

The teacher called my mom and dad and told

*them that I had played hooky, left school without
permission, and told a lie.*

*I was punished at home. It felt so unfair. I was
really innocent. Now, yes, I was extremely stupid,
but I was innocent!*

*For years I have remembered that incident.
I've nursed a hidden spot of resentment and anger
in my heart all this time, not just at the school and
the teacher and the principal, but at my dad because he believed them and punished me.*

*In fact, now, as an adult, I know I really was
wrong, in my own way. I did play hooky. Perhaps
my punishment was fair after all.*

*What matters now is that I still remember all
the anger that I had as a child. I may have been
young, but I had some very strong feelings of anger.*

*And you know what that makes me want to do?
I want to apply my memories of those feelings to my
daughter, Allison. I want to use my childhood memories for insight with my own child. Maybe through my
memories, I can feel some of the things she's feeling.*

Try to remember what it was like the first time you got
pushed around by a school bully. Try to remember what it felt
like when the teacher gave you so much homework that you

despaired of ever getting it done. Try to remember what it was like when your mom insisted on you wearing a certain pair of pants that you knew were out of style, how you went to school wearing them and all the kids laughed at you.

Sometimes life brings to a parent a little serendipity—an unexpected pleasure—with a child, which becomes an opportunity.

My dad was a master plumber. Some of my greatest days were spent helping him. He challenged me to learn common sense. The hours together formed a foundation for my life.

When my dad died, I felt so proud of what he had done. He taught me honesty, *hard, hard* work, trust in God and fairness toward people.

I will tell stories about him and my childhood as long as I can speak.

Lessons from childhood return to me every day. I can deal with a bully now because I had to deal with them in high school. I can work with disappointment because I had to as a child.

Those lessons still teach me as I teach my children and the thousands of people I speak to every year.

Never forget what you learned early in your life. The lessons, so often, still work.

Try to use those memories to experience some of what your children are feeling in their own lives.

The Teachable Moment

Sometimes life brings to a parent a little serendipity—an unexpected pleasure—with a child, which becomes an opportunity. We call these "teachable moments"—times when there is a chance to teach a child something valuable and profound.

This happened to Ron when Allison's dog suddenly died. The dog had a heat stroke. It was a bizarre, unexpected incident. Ron was nearly as upset as Allison was. He realized, however, that this tragedy offered him an opportunity with Allison—a teachable moment where whatever he told her would take root in her heart.

Ron told her something he had heard Robert Schuller say: "When you lose something, don't concentrate on what you lost—concentrate on what you have left." He encouraged Allison to think about all the good, happy memories she'd had with the dog. He told her to think about all the good friends and relatives that she had—people who loved her.

Ron had experienced a teachable moment. Chances are, Allison will remember that time and it will help her deal with other losses later in life.

*You need to
be ready for
the teachable
moment when
the heart of
your child is
unusually open.*

When you encounter one of these moments, the door is open, and anything you put into the doorway your child will accept. But if you let that moment pass, and the door slams in your face, then it's like trying to force a notebook under a closed door. You need to be ready for the teachable moment when the heart of your child is unusually open.

Look for those precious moments.

The Importance of Showing Respect

One of the hardest things a parent has to do is to understand how to relate to a child without being condescending. Children are different from adults, obviously, but they need to be given the same respect and dignity that adults are given. By showing respect to your child you give them an invisible hug. You're saying, "You're important to me."

One way to show respect is by listening. Someone once said, "Lend a child your ears, and you will open a pathway to her heart." Listening is not just a matter of acknowledging. Too many parents become busy with their own things, and when their child needs a listening ear, the parent nods absently, or grunts a passing acknowledgment. That's not listening. The child needs to know that you are paying attention.

The mistake we all make is thinking that what's important is what the child is wanting us to hear. The words of the child and the matters that are important to him may not really be that significant to us as adults. What matters in this situation is that the child see his parent put down his own business and pay attention to the need of the child.

It's not always what is being communicated verbally that the parent needs to listen to. It's the personhood of the child.

It's not always what is being communicated verbally that the parent needs to listen to. It's the personhood of the child. What is ultimately important is that the child understand that his parent respects him enough to listen.

Another way to show respect is by being approachable. Are you like a telephone—every time your child dials your number, he or she gets a busy signal? *Beep, beep, beep.* Does your child ever really get through?

Be approachable with your children. You make appointments, schedules, plans with adults. Do you do the same with your child? If your child is as important to you as your business associates, then you ought to.

Unfortunately, an appointment with a child is the one appointment most easily broken, because the child has no immediate power to make you keep the appointment. But the child retains a memory of broken appointments and may later in life pay you back with rebellion. An adolescent remembers broken contracts.

> *Your lifelong mission is not to punish your children into maturity, but to cultivate their maturity throught love and respect.*

So make yourself approachable. Make appointments with your children. And make sure you keep those appointments.

Third, show respect for your child by offering forgiveness. Realize that your child feels the sting and pain of wrong behavior just as much as you feel as an adult. You know that when you blow it as an adult, the thing that you need desperately is for the person you wronged to put his arm around you and say, "I forgive you." Your children need the same thing. Let your children know that you really do forgive them. If you can do this, you'll make it easier for them to understand and receive the forgiveness they need from God. They can learn forgiveness through a loving mom and dad. You see, your lifelong mission is not to punish your children into maturity, but to cultivate their maturity through love and respect.

The Law of Sowing and Reaping

One of the most loving things you can teach your children is the simple truth that in life you will reap what you sow.

Ron has a favorite quote by Ralph Waldo Emerson:

This law of consequences is the law that writes the other laws of cities and nations. It will not be balked of its end in the smallest iota. It is in vain to build or to plot or combine against this law of consequences. Life invests itself with inevitable conditions which the unwise seek to dodge. If a man escapes these consequences in one part, they will attack him in another more vital part. If he escapes them in form and appearance, it is that he has resisted his life and fled from himself, and the retribution is so much death. All things are doubled, there are trade-offs for everything—one against the other, tit for tat, an eye for an eye, give and it shall be given to you, he that watereth shall be watered himself. What will you have? This is what God says: pay for it and take it. It is thus written because that is the way it is in life.

That's nineteenth-century English, but let me put it into everyday language for you. It simply means that you can't get away from consequences. You must always be oriented toward the future. You should always be thinking: *If I do this today, what will happen tomorrow?*

I have tried with God's help to sow right principles into my children since their earliest days.

Three of my sons—Doyle, Jeff, and Steve—help run my business operations. They have great talent, and they lead in ways consistent with my goals. My other children—Dexter, Jr., April, Lisa, and Leanne—all contribute to Christian causes individually and at different times have helped with some of my business endeavors.

Both Birdie and I have tried to sow well and are now reaping great personal and spiritual rewards from our children.

Remember the verses in the Bible?

Don't be misled; remember that you can't ignore God and get away with it: a man will always reap just the kind of crop he sows! If he sows to please his own wrong desires, he will be planting seeds of evil and he will surely reap a harvest of spiritual decay and death; but if he plants the good things of the Spirit, he will reap the everlasting life that the Holy Spirit gives him.

This is a great principle to teach children.

A Relationship with Jesus Christ

The best hug you can give your children is a relationship with Jesus Christ.

Of course, this starts with you. Through your own willingness to turn from your sin and your selfishness, you become an example to your children. You have to show them that you can't rely on your church or your baptism or your goodness to make you a Christian, but that your Christianity is a relationship with Jesus Christ. In the Bible, the apostle Paul says in writing to a group of early Christians, "Follow me as I follow Jesus Christ." You may feel terribly unworthy of that responsibility. Join the club—we all are. But with God's

> *Through your own willingness to turn from your sin and your selfishness, you become an example to your children.*

help you can do it. Look at your children and make this verse your guide, your motivator. Say to your children, "You follow me and I'll try to follow Jesus Christ." In that way, they will learn to follow and love and know Jesus Christ personally. The greatest joy you will ever know will be when you get to heaven someday, and looking around you, you see that your children are there.

Nothing in the world is of greater importance. It's the ultimate hug.

Chapter 8

BECOMING A WINNER IN BUSINESS

In previous books I have written about the importance of achieving financial independence. Here are several reasons why this is important.

First, it gives you freedom from the petty problems of life. The little things of daily life—car repair, dental bills, unexpected expenses—are not as frustrating or difficult when you have the money to cover them and when they're already built into your financial plan. You don't have to worry so much about the frustrating details of daily life. Second, it builds into your character a greater sense of self-respect. Financial independence makes you your own boss. In the process of creating your own business, you get a self-esteem boost. Third, it can provide you dignity and security in your old age. As we mentioned earlier in this book, planning for your financial future after retirement is a daunting task. If you're financially free and have a business working for you, you have greater resources to face the future.

Your financial independence, however, is important not just for you, but also for your family. Financial independence will do several things for your wife and children. First, it will relieve your marriage of financial conflict. Counselors say that one of the primary conflicts in marriage is over finances. People get divorced sometimes just because they never could agree about how to handle money. Financial independence can relieve some of this tension. Second, it will allow you to provide adequately for your children. The cost of a college education is enormous these days, increasing at a rate of 12 percent a year. If you are financially independent, you should have more resources to use in helping your children through school or in pursuing a career. Third, it will allow you to be an example to your family and instill in them the proper understanding of money and financial success. Being the financial leader in your home is a treasured, heroic role for you to play. If you are financially free, your wife and children will look up to you in a new way.

Building your own business is a real battle—if you've started making the effort to get out of debt, you know how hard it is! It takes hard work, lots of self-discipline, and persistence to become financially free and graduate to the position of being your own boss. So it's a real war, a series of

> *Your financial independence is important not just for you, but also for your family.*

battles that must be won if you are to truly be a hero to your family. But the rewards are significant, not only for you but for your family as well.

Success Secrets

What is it that makes certain people succeed in business in spectacular ways? How is it that some people seem to rise above the competition and achieve greater things than anyone else? Why do some people take on a difficult business enterprise and manage to achieve great success?

More than anything, it's an attitude. Ron and I have written frequently about the subject of character. That's no accident. It's the fundamental difference between those who have won the battle for financial independence and those who have lost. It takes depth of character for a man to succeed in business on his own, to become financially free.

In the next few pages we'd like to offer seven character tips for the struggle ahead—the fight for your financial freedom.

1. Avoid the crybaby mentality. Today everyone is a victim. In bookstores today there is a category of literature called "recovery books." These books tell you how you've become a victim—say, of alcoholism, a bad family, of religion, of childhood abuse, etc.—and how you can overcome those problems. You don't even have to experience these things directly—if your wife or a friend experiences them, you still may be a victim through something called codependency.

> *If you want to develop the attitude you'll need to be a hero in business, you can't let yourself think like a victim.*

There is a need for some of these books, and the concepts being taught here can be helpful. But what's disturbing about this particular movement of self-help psychology is how it teaches everyone that he or she is a victim. When you think of yourself as a victim, you suddenly have an excuse for your failure.

Look at what we call "dysfunctional" families. It is popular today to talk about how you came from a dysfunctional family and how you can't help your behavior. You may be messed up in your marriage and fouled up in your finances, but you can say, "I'm from a dysfunctional family," and that supposedly explains everything.

Well, the term *dysfunctional* may be a new one, but it's an old reality. Ronald Reagan talks of his troubled childhood in his autobiography. He would come home at night and frequently would have to pick up his dad off the floor because his dad was in a drunken stupor. He speaks of the vivid embarrassment caused by his father's humiliating behavior. But somewhere along the line Ronald Reagan said, "I'll not be a victim of that." He chose not to be a victim of a bad situation.

Abraham Lincoln had such a dysfunctional relationship with his own father that when his father died, Lincoln refused to go to the funeral. He wouldn't speak to the man who helped give him life, and yet Abraham Lincoln became a giant of world power and a true American hero.

If you want to develop the attitude you'll need to be a hero in business, you can't let yourself think like a victim. You can't look backward all your life. You have to focus on the future.

Yes, you may need therapeutic counsel to overcome the past, but you don't need sympathy and excuses.

What are you going to do with your life from now on? That's the essential question.

2. *Fight fairness frustration.* This is the popular mind-set today—that if something goes wrong in your life, it ought not to have happened. It assumes that you have a right to fairness in life. We think this attitude has been particularly common among the yuppie generation, people who've grown up with many advantages and opportunities, but who've generally been spoiled. They expect so much to come to them so easily. They expect life to be fair.

Unfortunately life isn't.

Life frequently deals you a bad hand. Those people who moan about the hand they've been dealt will never succeed. It's those who make the best of the cards they hold who are the ones to accomplish much in business.

Writers trying to get their books published are frequently dealt a bad hand when they get rejection slips from publishers. But those writers who become successful are those who persevere, not those who complain about how unfair it is that a publisher doesn't spend enough time with their manuscript. I'm told of one British novelist, John Creasey, has published 564 books. You could say he's fought and won the battle for his business. You see, he didn't sell his first manuscript until after he had received some 774 rejection slips.

3. Stop being a brooder reactor. You've probably heard about nuclear breeder reactors? This is a nuclear reactor that breeds more material to be used in other nuclear products.

A human brooder reactor is one who reacts and broods, producing a lot of negative material to pass around to others.

If you have a melancholy mentality, you'll never become a winner in business.

Ron and his family were at Disney World some time ago. Allison was going to take a class at MGM studios. They went up to the gate, and the man at the gate was in a bad mood. Now generally the people at Disney are absolutely great, but this man apparently was an exception. He wouldn't let them in, even though it was the gate they were supposed to be going through. Eventually they went to another gate and got in.

Now Ron let that bad experience get to him. He reacted and brooded. It was a beautiful morning. There were flowers blooming in the Disney gardens, and Ron was about to spend the whole day alone with his wife, Amy. But Ron just brooded over what that man had said to him. Finally Amy said, "Are you going to ruin our day because of a total stranger?" Ron woke up from being a brooder reactor and was able to salvage the day.

You can't be a brooder reactor and build a successful business. "You will never do well when you tend to dwell."

4. Don't allow yourself to get down on yourself. Some people are drawn to the dark side of life. They actually love living in gloom.

Are you like this? Do you love to ponder the painful and pathetic? Do you love to think of all the reasons your business will probably fail?

Ron tells about how he was like this earlier in his life. He grew up in an area of southeastern Kentucky. It was a backward area where the roads were frightfully primitive His hometown was a hundred miles from Lexington, Kentucky, but it took almost six hours to get to Lexington by car because the road system was so bad.

The isolation of this region made it conducive to a death fixation. And Ron, growing up, developed a real crippling fear of death. It ate at him, haunted him, followed him, and worked against his success because it consumed his thinking. He would think, *You work hard and then you die.* It's all he could think about.

Ron tells about how he was able to overcome his tendency toward depression thinking:

> *I wish I could tell you some great psychological maneuver that rescued me from that situation, but*

it wasn't. It was this: I had the most incredible personal experience with Jesus Christ. That set me free from my fear of death. When Jesus Christ came into my life and released his power to change me from the inside out, my fear of death began to go away.

I remember once walking in a cemetery with my wife, Amy, and she said, "Ron, you still have lingering fear here. You need to ask God to help you. The same Jesus Christ who died for you and rose from the dead and lives in your heart is going to welcome you into heaven someday, and you don't have to be afraid."

It was like a light went off in my head, and I realized that this fear was useless. I don't know where you're going to be in five hundred years, but I'm going to be doing something great in the presence of God because of Jesus Christ.

I, also, have learned to overcome negative thinking. I am not someone who thinks about the negative a lot. But there are times when I'm concerned for my family's future—when I worry about dying and leaving them. That's when I trust God. I've worked hard to provide financial security, and I "trust hard" for God to take care of them. My favorite passage of Scripture for the protection of my family is Psalm 91. I pray it and stand on it every day.

If you have depression thinking, you'll never become a winner in business. It will pull you down and make you less effective in life, with your family, and with your friends. Whatever the noose is around your neck, cut yourself free and find God's way to overcome your fears.

5. Don't be ruled by the need for other people's approval. You can't build great success if you are addicted to other people's approval.

Many people don't realize how much they depend on "people-pleasing" to run their lives. They make decisions based on whether they see the nod of the head or the smile on a face or hear a voice of approval. It can be a very subtle thing.

It's a weakness to make decisions based on people's approval. The people around you won't always be right. And when the people around you change, then your decision will change too—you'll become indecisive.

I've counseled Ron personally about this problem. He told me of his encounter with people-pleasing when he was in Alabama:

I was speaking at a Methodist church. The pastor, who is a good friend of mine to this day, said

*something that could have been construed as a
criticism. Now I don't think he intended it that way.
But I lay awake all night worrying that he didn't
like what I did.*

*Eventually God rescued me through Amy, as
he has done so frequently in my life. Amy said,
"What's troubling you?"*

*I told her, and she said, "Are you called of
God or not? You'll never be a spiritual leader if
you have to feed on that man's approval."*

And I immediately prayed to be released from it.

We believe that this problem of people-pleasing can
paralyze you into indecision. If you want to be successful
in business, then you can no longer allow your life to be
haunted by the overdependent need for other people's
approval.

6. Overcome personal cowardice. There's an old English word for cowardice—it's the word *craven*. Some British plays and novels from the seventeenth and eighteenth
centuries refer to people as craven individuals—men or
women who chose cowardice when they could have been
brave. Built into the very word was the sense that it was
impossible to respect someone who had chosen to be cow-
ardly.

It takes courage to build your business. The battles are fierce; the rate of failure is high. If you have a pattern of personal cowardice inside you, you'll never succeed.

Your battle for financial freedom is very much a battle— and you need to develop the personal courage to see it through, to weather the setbacks, and to see if those needed resources are deep inside you.

We believe one of the reasons that personal cowardice is an issue today is that many of us have not had recent models of real courage in our life. The Persian Gulf War in 1991 was one exception. We saw how America's men and women fought brilliantly and valiantly to overcome Saddam Hussein and his forces. Seeing our soldiers overcome their personal fears and triumph courageously is a motivation to us all.

But generally we have lacked these models of courage in our life. Perhaps that's why many people today struggle with fears, cowardice, and timidity in making business decisions.

One story going back to the beginning of the century still stands as a shining example of great courage.

Charles Whittlesy was a young dentist from New York

City who was drafted in World War I. He went to France for his education, and he emerged from school as a refined, distinguished gentleman.

He went to war with a distaste for everything it represented, but he had a profound sense of duty to his country. He quickly became a major, commanding a battalion. Toward the end of the war, in the northern part of France, he led his men in a mad, daring dash into enemy lines. They penetrated far behind enemy defenses, but suddenly found themselves lost, cut off, and almost certain to be annihilated by the German forces closing in rapidly around them. They had lost any hope of retreat.

Major Whittlesy gathered his wit and courage and began to develop in his men the desire to fight valiantly. They became known in the next few weeks as the "lost battalion." Newspapers reported the story, and people back home prayed for the deliverance of the lost battalion.

They lost more than two-thirds of their men. One of Whittlesy's officers was severely wounded by the German "potato masher"—a long wooden stick with a cylinder at the top full of explosives. When the potato masher exploded in his face, the wooden handle split off and struck him in the side. He couldn't pull the wood out of his side, so he fought for the next week with this wood protruding from his ribs, stopping the bleeding only by applying pressure every few minutes as he fought off the Germans.

The battalion had a cage with two carrier pigeons. The men took one pigeon and, in the attempt to get the bird off, sent it with wrong coordinates for the Allied artillery. The pigeon got through, but with this wrong information. The U.S. artillery commander issued the orders, and the lost battalion was soon hammered by friendly fire. Still the lost battalion held out.

The battalion had one more pigeon. But this bird was so frightened by the artillery, it flew up, landed in a tree, and refused to go anywhere. One man, risking his life, climbed to the top of the tree and coaxed the pigeon into the air. With that, the pigeon finally made it through to the Allies, this time with the correct coordinates. The battalion—what was left of it—was rescued.

War, as terrible as it is, forces us to find resources inside ourselves we never knew were there. Your battle for financial freedom is very much a battle—and you need to develop the personal courage to see it through, to weather the setbacks, and to find those needed resources within you.

We like the quote by Maxwell Maltz: "We must have the courage to bet on our ideas, to take the calculated risk, and to act. Everyday living requires courage if life is to be effective and bring happiness."

To win in business, you need to overcome personal cowardice and find the resources of courage within you.

7. Let your business be ruled by God. It seems fitting to close the book on this point because we believe it's the most important factor in fighting and winning all the battles in your life. You'll never be a hero to anyone until you recognize the spiritual dimension of your life and give yourself to God. True success is found only through him.

When I was a young man, I came to a solid, fulfilling relationship with Jesus Christ as my personal Savior.

Since then my love for my family has only strengthened my love for Christ. Birdie has been a consistent, positive spiritual influence. Her prayers and encouragement have often boosted my growth. I pray for my children and grand-children. I talk with them about the reality of Jesus Christ and the necessity of a living relationship with him.

The success of my marriage and family life is due to this relationship with Christ and the power of the Holy Spirit working in the life of each one of us.

Ron came to know Jesus Christ personally as a teenager. That same love of God that motivates me is also present in Ron. The happiness and fulfillment that Ron has in both his marriage and family is founded on biblical living and on a relationship with Jesus Christ.

The good news here is that neither of us enjoy this spiritual dimension because we are unusually good and religious men. We experience Christ in our lives because we have accepted his death on the cross for us. We experience what is freely available to you, if you wish to receive Christ as your Savior and surrender your life to him.

In saying this, we are sensitive to those of you who are of other religions. You may be Jewish, Buddhist, Hindu, or Muslim. We mean you no offense. Our purpose, rather, is to communicate the power and reality of the living Christ, who has himself given us the help that has produced our happy homes.

In gratitude to Christ and in love for you we share this message.

God bless you!

Don't Let Anybody Steal Your Dream
Dexter Yager with Doug Wead

This classic in the field of motivational writing has sold more than a million copies and is selling as well today as it did in 1978 when it was first published. Dexter Yager has influenced millions with his forthright honesty, compassion and desire to see others succeed. Here is a man who has "made it" in all the right ways, and who is willing to pour out the ideas that make for successful living.

BK10 English Paperback
IBK1 Spanish Paperback
IBK7 French Paperback
IBK16 Dutch Paperback
IBK21 German Paperback

The Secret of Living Is Giving
Birdie Yager with Gloria Wead

Birdie Yager, wife of one of America's most famous and powerful businessmen, talks about:
- Marriage: How to make it work.
- Attitude: The way to popularity and self-esteem.
- Your Husband: How to make him rich!
- Children: When to say no, and when to say yes.
- Health and Beauty: They are result of our decisions, and are not automatic.
- Money: When it is bad; when it can be wonderful.
- Faith in God: Why you must deal with your guilt and inferiority, or self-destruct.

BK96 English Paperback
IBK24 Spanish Paperback
IBK22 French Paperback
IBK25 German Paperback

Becoming Rich
Dexter Yager and Doug Wead

Inspirational and moving stories of some of the world's greatest people and the eleven principles behind their success. Includes Walt Disney, Albert Einstein, Martin Luther King, Andrew Carnegie, Adolph Ochs, Jackie Robinson, Thomas Edison, Helen Keller, Harry Truman, Coco Chanel, Winston Churchill, Arturo Toscanini, and Douglas MacArthur.
BK97 English Paperback

Millionaire Mentality
Dexter Yager with Doug Wead

At last! A book on financial responsibility by one of America's financial wizards, Dexter Yager! Dexter gives freely of his remarkable business acumen, teaching you how to take inventory and plan for financial independence.

Here is a common sense, down-to-earth book about investments, shopping, credit and car buying, and budgeting time and money.

Included are anecdotes about other successful American business people—to give you ideas about where to go from here!

If you are serious about financial planning, this is the book for you!
BK206 English Paperback

A Millionaire's Common-Sense Approach to Wealth
Dexter Yager with Ron Ball

Financial principles on which to build your life and your dream. Based on Dexter Yager's own life-tested success secrets, this book provides valuable instruction and direction for those who are just beginning to get a vision for success. Learn common misconceptions people have about money and materialism; Discover the eleven reasons to be rich (some may surprise you!); read about the five keys to financial prosperity— the dream principle, work principle, perseverance principle, investment principle, and people principle; break down the budget barriers in your own life; and learn common sense perspectives on managing money. This book will help you turn your life around.
BK315 English Paperback

The Business Handbook (1993 Revised Edition)
Dexter Yager with Doyle Yager

This is it: The most comprehensive how-to-do-it book ever offered for building your Amway business!

Unleash the proven success system with this easy-to-read guide which details the way to CHART YOUR OWN PATH toward achievement.

The Business Handbook, now featuring over 400 pages filled with strategies, illustrations, quotations and proven patterns, brings you the finest, proven techniques for **anyone**—from a new distributor to a seasoned veteran—who desires to build a larger, more profitable, highly motivated organization.

Best of all, *The Business Handbook* helps provide you with the latest growth-oriented, validated information.

Understand the historic relationships between direct selling, network marketing and interactive distribution.

Learn the distinct, powerful differences between our corporate sponsor's time-proven sales and marketing plan and other "just-like-Amway-only-better" would-be companies.

Prepare to tap into the phenomenon known as interactive distribution.

Develop yourself for future success by learning about:
- Winning
- Leadership
- Goalsetting
- Dreambuilding
- Loyalty
- Mentor Relationships
- Paradigms
- Trends in Distribution
- International Sponsoring
- Using the Latest Tools

Above all, discover the powerful pattern for success, empowerment and fulfillment used by hundreds of Amway Diamonds!

BK247 English Paperback

Successful Family Ties: Developing Right Relationships for Lasting Success
Ron Ball with Dexter Yager

Right relationships with the people around you are fundamental to your success in life—emotionally, spiritually, and even in your work. This book will give you high-performance, practical guidelines for dealing with the many important issues that may be holding you back from experiencing success in your family relationships. You'll learn to recognize the signs of trouble and to take steps toward overcoming:
- ruptured relationships
- busy signals in communication
- sexual temptation
- stress
- negative people

And with principles founded on God-given, timeless truths you'll discover lasting success in all your challenges and be sure to have successful family ties.

BK310 English Paperback

Mark of a Millionaire
Dexter Yager and Ron Ball

Character principles that will change your life. Develop the traits that are common to successful business people. From becoming a dreamer to being hard-working, from overcoming fears to seeking good counsel, from becoming a pioneer to establishing yourself as a person of integrity—these classic character principles are the foundation for success.

BK334 English Paperback

Everything I Know at the Top
I Learned at the Bottom
Dexter Yager and Ron Ball

Personal stories and lessons from the life of Dexter Yager provide insights into the keys to success. Read about Dexter Yager's early boyhood experiences selling soda pop to construction workers; learn the important business principle he picked up from his early days selling cars. Out of these personal accounts from the life of a successful leader, you can learn valuable lessons for use in your career and your life.

BK351 English Paperback

Ordinary Men, Extraordinary Heroes
Dexter Yager and Ron Ball

Essential advice for winning the war for your family. Discover how the forces of our culture are trying to destroy your relationship with your wife and kids. Learn how to avoid infidelity. Discover the strategies for hugging your kids. Read seven ways you can win in the battle for your business.

BK380 English Paperback

*Available from your distributor,
local bookstore, or write to:*

*Internet Services Corporation
P.O. Box 412080
Charlotte, NC 28241-2080*